W9-DDH-919

Responding to Loss

A Resource for Caregivers

Adolf Hansen

Death, Value and Meaning Series
Series Editor: John D. Morgan

Baywood Publishing Company, Inc.
AMITYVILLE, NEW YORK

Copyright © 2004 by Baywood Publishing Company, Inc., Amityville, New York

Baywood Publishing Company, Inc.
26 Austin Avenue
Amityville, NY 11701
(800) 638-7819
E-mail: baywood@baywood.com
Web site: baywood.com

Library of Congress Catalog Number: 2004047692
ISBN: 0-89503-301-1 (cloth)

Library of Congress Cataloging-in-Publication Data

Hansen, Adolf, 1938
    Responding to loss : a resource for caregivers / Adolf Hansen.
        p. cm. -- (Death, value, and meaning series)
    Includes bibliographical references and index.
    ISBN 0-89503-301-1 (cloth)
        1. Loss (Psychology). 2. Grief. 3. Bereavement--Psychological aspects. 4.
    Death--Psychological aspects. 5. Attachment behavior. 6. Counseling. I. Title. II. Series

BF575.D35H35 2004
155.9'3--dc22
                                                                    2004047692

**DEDICATED TO THE THREE
MOST IMPORTANT PERSONS IN MY LIFE**

NAOMI, my wife
who exemplifies incredible faith, hope, and love
in all she does

BECKY, our daughter
who wasn't supposed to live, but did

BONNIE, our daughter
who wasn't supposed to die, but did

Contents

Preface

This volume sets forth an approach for dealing with loss experiences, particularly those losses that are brought about by breaks in attachments. It assumes that all persons have attachments, breaks in attachments, and experiences of loss that emerge from these breaks.

The focus of this approach lies in three key premises: 1) that there is in every functioning human being a freedom to respond to her or his circumstance; 2) that there is a challenge to use this freedom in a responsible manner; and 3) that there is a resultant transformation that inevitably takes place. This focus is filled with potential for profound meaning, since there are resources available to all persons for a basically positive response and transformation.

The understanding that is the basis for this approach has primarily grown out of research, teaching, and personal experience in the subject of death and dying. Research has included reading the works of others in this specific area as well as in a variety of related fields. It has also developed through conferring with professional colleagues in educational, clinical, and religious settings. It has become most crystallized in the interaction with persons in individual interviews and counseling sessions as well as in group teaching and learning experiences.

Teaching has included courses at the University of Indianapolis while I was serving as Professor and Chair of the Department of Philosophy and Religion, particularly a course entitled "The Meaning of Death" that was offered a number of times. During the years there I also taught a course at Indiana University School of Medicine entitled "Death, Grief, and Bereavement." In more recent years, while serving as Associate Professor and Vice President for Administration at Garrett-Evangelical Theological Seminary, I have taught a course entitled "Loss and Grief." In addition, I have led numerous continuing education events for caregivers, both laity and clergy, in educational institutions, hospitals, agencies, local churches, ecclesiastical bodies, and other professional contexts.

Personal experience beyond these research and teaching settings has included deaths in my immediate family. My father died in 1980 after a long and difficult bout with lung cancer (even though he never smoked). My mother died a relatively peaceful death in 1991 following a series of physical problems. My sister—my only sibling—died in 1996 after a tumultuous struggle with numerous illnesses, the last being a failure in kidney function.

Yet, beyond any anguish I had ever known was the sudden and violent death of my daughter, Bonnie, in 1996. She was struck by a bus in downtown Indianapolis on Friday afternoon, May 10th. She had just left her office at a national firm, where she worked as an attorney. She walked to the street corner and saw the light was red. She waited. When the light turned green, she entered the pedestrian walkway. When she was more than halfway across, a bus driver (who has been found to be at fault) turned her bus into the walkway and struck her. Injuries from a blow to her head caused her never to regain consciousness. Bonnie was pronounced dead at 6:15 P.M. the next day, Saturday, my birthday, the eve of Mother's Day.

In the years preceding Bonnie's death there were also the repeated, life-threatening circumstances of my other daughter, Becky. They began one February afternoon in 1976, at age 14, with a visit to her pediatrician due to headaches and double vision. Referral was made to a neurosurgeon. A few days later she was in the hospital undergoing tests. A diagnosis was given that indicated the likelihood of a blockage in the ventricular system of the brain. Surgery was scheduled and lasted for over 11 hours. The blockage couldn't be removed. A shunt was installed. Medications were prescribed.

The recuperation was very long, both physically and emotionally. It went on for months. Complications set in. A second surgery was scheduled, followed by a third and a fourth. During 1974, 1975, and 1976 a total of nine major surgeries took place. Many weeks were spent in intensive care. Death came very close, over and over again. At one point tentative funeral plans were made as doctors indicated that there didn't seem to be anything further that could be done. Yet Becky never gave up and eventually made a remarkable and full recovery.

Throughout all the years when there were deaths or near-death experiences in my immediate family, there were also countless interactions with a variety of individuals and groups dealing with experiences of death and dying, as well as numerous other experiences of loss. Each of them contributed to the understanding delineated in this volume. Most helpful were the interactions with family members, close friends, and professional colleagues, as well as with students and faculty at the University of Indianapolis, Indiana University School of Medicine, Garrett-Evangelical Theological Seminary, and Northwestern University.

Those who read all or part of this manuscript prior to publication made many useful comments that contributed significantly to its final formulation. I deeply appreciate their insights. They include Becky and Rick Arnott, Diane and Don Carlson, Kenneth Doka, Neal Fisher, Leah Gunning, David Hogue, Joey Lenti, Robert Neimeyer, Thomas Petty, James Poling, Michael St. Pierre, Lallene Rector, Dennis Sasso, Herman Schaalman, Patrick Skinner, Joan Snelz, Sharon Van Divier, and John Wimmer. I am also very grateful for the assistance provided to me by colleagues at Baywood, especially Stuart Cohen, John Morgan, Bobbi Olszewski, and Julie Krempa.

I owe a profound debt of gratitude to two persons who were incredibly important to me in this process, my assistant, Sally Blackwell, and my wife, Naomi Hansen. Without their wisdom, assistance, and support, this book would never have been written.

Much of what has been learned is included in this volume. It is expressed in the form of both analysis and illustration. Each of the examples comes out of a real-life situation, although they have been modified in ways that protect the identity of the persons who are involved.

With a need to set parameters, there are five topics that are related to the subject of this volume, but are not dealt with in detail. The first one is the establishing of attachments during infancy and childhood years. This is very important; however, the focal point in this examination is with adults who already have a number of attachments that have been developed over a period of years. How they came to be during infancy, childhood, and adolescence is mentioned, yet that is not what is primary.

A second topic that does not receive specific attention is the breaking of basically negative attachments. The concentration is on attachments that are, overall, positive and on breaks that are, overall, negative. This does not mean that negative attachments are not significant. Quite the contrary. Yet the scope of this analysis is not that inclusive.

A third area that is not included is the breaking of basically non-conscious attachments. The focus is on attachments that are known to the individual. This is also the case with breaks. Those attachments that are preconscious, subconscious, and/or unconscious are beyond the scope of this book, except as the individual becomes aware of them.

A fourth issue that is not given detailed attention, although it is identified, is the unhealthy or morbid responses that are sometimes made to breaks in attachments. Investigating such responses would entail a very lengthy analysis, since there are so many ways this can be done and these ways are often so complex. The attention in this volume is given to responses that are essentially healthy and wholesome.

A fifth topic that emerges from the former is the transformation that sometimes takes place in primarily negative ways. That is, the end result of a long-term series of morbid responses may eventuate in a personality that is substantially pathological. Such a pursuit is, once again, beyond the scope of this study. Instead, the focus is on transformation that is substantially positive.

It is to the ends that have been articulated in this introduction, and to the restricted scope that has also been identified, that this volume is directed. It is hoped that persons who read it and reflect on it will learn how to respond to loss experiences in their own lives in ways that are emotionally healthy, intellectually coherent, spiritually genuine, culturally sensitive, relationally authentic, and personally fulfilling. It is also hoped that persons who relate to others as caregivers—both as professionals and non-professionals—will find ways to help others learn how to respond to loss experiences.

To live is to experience loss.

To survive is to learn how to respond.

CHAPTER 1

Possibilities for Meaning: Attachments

In life there are numerous possibilities for meaning. They often grow out of a reflection on life in which individuals: first, identify those attachments that really matter at the present time; second, relate them to previous experiences; and third, decide how to develop them in the future.

Central to these attachments are relationships, many of which are with other persons. However, there are also relationships with things (physical objects), places (locations), events (actual occurrences), and a variety of intangibles (a certain type of music, a perception of beauty, a dream, a sense of humor, etc.).

Every functioning human being has relationships in each of these categories; however, the nature of those relationships varies from one individual to another. Yet the most significant for virtually all persons is relationships with other persons. It consists of both feelings (emotional ties) and thoughts (intellectual formulations), with feelings more influential for some, and thoughts more influential for others.

Infant and childhood experiences are the most crucial in the development of such relationships, particularly in the establishing of attachments. John Bowlby formulated the basic framework for the approach that he and others have called "attachment theory." He sets forth this perspective in three volumes that he entitles *Attachment and Loss* (1969, 1973, 1980). The most crucial tenets, taken from a more detailed outline [1, pp. 39-41], are summarized in the paragraphs that follow.

1

First, attachment behavior is understood as any form of behavior that results in an individual attaining or retaining proximity to another person who is clearly identifiable and who is distinctively preferred. The proximity, or closeness to another person, takes time and energy, not only to develop, but also to maintain. It emerges when the other person is plainly differentiated and decidedly more desirable [2].

Second, attachment behavior leads to the development of attachments that become affectional bonds if that development occurs in a basically healthy manner. This takes place initially between a child and his or her parent(s) or primary caregiver(s) and later between an adult and an adult. Conversely, if the development is basically unhealthy, the affectional bonds may emerge in only a minimal manner, or may not emerge at all.

Third, the formation, maintenance, disruption, and renewal of attachments give rise to many of the most intense emotions that human beings experience. Throughout these four movements inherent in the cycle of life, there exist not only the broad range of feelings, but also the most penetrating depth of feelings, whether they are in the arena of gladness and joy, of anguish and anger, or sadness and pain.

Fourth, attachment behavior in an adult is not necessarily indicative of a fixation at, or a regression to, an earlier, immature stage of development—a point of view set forth by some on the basis of conceptualizations that derive from theories of orality and dependency. Neither is attachment behavior indicative of some form of pathology.

Fifth, the most important determinants of the pathway along which an individual's attachment behavior develops are the experiences he or she has with attachment figures during the years of infancy and childhood, and, to a lesser extent, adolescence. These experiences also shape the pattern in which the attachment behavior becomes organized.

Sixth, the way in which an individual's attachment behavior becomes organized within his or her personality determines—to a large extent—the pattern of affectional bonds he or she makes throughout life. To understand such an organization, and the ways it has developed, however, not only informs an individual of the likelihood of patterns that may emerge, but also provides opportunities for the individual to affirm, modify, or acquiesce to such patterns.

Further expression of this paradigm was carried out by Mary Ainsworth, particularly in the volume, *Patterns of Attachment: A Psychological Study of the Strange Situation,* in which she focuses on the attachment of infants to their mother figures, utilizing empirical data to compare and contrast relationships between behavior in "the strange situation" and at home [3].

In a more recent article, Ainsworth moves beyond infancy in understanding attachment. In doing so she deals with long-lasting interpersonal relationships that, at times, involve affectional bonds [4, pp. 33-51]. She distinguishes these affectional bonds from rela- tionships by indicating: 1) that relationships are necessarily twofold, while bonds can be characteristic of an individual; 2) that relation- ships may be long-term or brief, while bonds are by definition long-term; and 3) that relationships between individuals grow out of the development of varied interactions, some of which do not pertain to an affectional bond. In order to clarify her distinctions, she defines an affectional bond as "a relatively long-enduring tie in which a partner is important as a unique individual, interchangeable with none other" [4, p. 37].

A number of other researchers have also made important con- tributions to the development of attachment theory. Conferences in London in 1981 and 1988 were each summarized in separate volumes. The first, *The Place of Attachment in Human Behavior,* brought a broader recognition to this paradigm [5]. It dealt with infant-mother attachment, problems in parenting, bonding in adult life, and disorders in adult life. The second, *Attachment Across the Life Cycle,* raised awareness even further [6]. It focused on the nature of attachment, patterns of attachment, and clinical applications.

A subsequent conference in Toronto in 1993 brought together researchers and clinicians to review the developing state of knowl- edge regarding attachment theory and practice. A book was pro- duced from that conference entitled *Attachment Theory: Social, Developmental, and Clinical Perspectives* [7].

Interest in producing an even broader, more representative collection eventuated in a volume in 1999 called *Handbook of Attachment: Theory, Research, and Clinical Applications* [8]. It brings the field up to date in a manner that combines an in-depth analysis and a comprehensive overview.

Many additional writings pertaining to attachment have emerged in the last decade of the 20th century and the early years of this century [9]. Three are particularly noteworthy since they relate attachment theory to other psychological approaches. The first one is the special issue of the *Journal of the American Psychoanalytic Association* in 2000 entitled "Psychoanalysis, Development and the Life Cycle" [10]. The collection of articles focuses on the dialog that is needed between psychoanalysis and attachment theory. In the words of the editors, "It seems it is time for rapprochement. Our hope is that with this publication more and better dialogue will take place, and that more psychoanalysts will begin to take account of the enormous contributions, as well as the challenges, that attachment theory can provide" [11, p. 1048].

The second is a volume by Peter Fonagy, *Attachment Theory and Psychoanalysis* [12]. It explores more fully the interactions between attachment theory and a range of psychoanalytical schools of thought, from Freud to the evolving relational or intersubjective approaches [12, pp. 123-134]. In this process, points of contact as well as divergence are noted. Throughout, there is an attempt to build bridges that will enable an integration of these approaches.

The third is a book by Jeremy Holmes, *The Search for the Secure Base: Attachment Theory and Psychotherapy* [13]. It sets forth a new paradigm in psychotherapy with adults, one that utilizes an attachment-informed therapy. Permeating this approach is the attempt to bring about a rapprochement between psychoanalysis and attachment theory. To assist in that process, a "brief attachment-based therapy" is delineated as a treatment modality [13, pp. 144-167].

Growing out of the development of attachment theory are numerous theoretical and clinical distinctions. Three rather straightforward ones that are utilized in this volume are: 1) that relationships are very significant in understanding human behavior; 2) that attachments involve particular kinds of relationships; and 3) that affectional bonds involve particular kinds of attachments. Whereas Bowlby uses attachments and affectional bonds interchangeably [1, p. 39; 2] and Ainsworth speaks of attachments as a certain type of affectional bond [4, p. 38], either of which can be properly defended, this analysis will deal with attachments in a broader sense and will speak of affectional bonds as a certain type of attachment.

These distinctions may be depicted in an image of three circles: the largest circle indicates relationships; the smaller circle within it signifies attachments; and the smallest circle at the center of the other two represents affectional bonds. The latter is identified by Bowlby in the words: "Intimate attachments to other human beings are the hub around which a person's life revolves, not only when he is an infant or a toddler or a schoolchild, but throughout his adolescence and his years of maturity as well, and on into old age" [1, p. 442].

In the utilization of attachment theory in this volume, the understanding of attachments is, therefore, broader in scope and more varied in intensity than the approach of Bowlby, Ainsworth, and others. Hopefully, this will place findings that already have been established in a larger context without negating the validity of the many views that have emerged. Attachments are understood to refer not only to persons, but also to material things, actual places, real life events, and a variety of intangibles. In this way, possibilities for meaning extend beyond attachments to other persons while, at the same time, such attachments remain as the core of one's meaning, at least for individuals with a reasonably healthy and mature disposition toward life.

Attachments in each of these categories are a combination of both positive and negative traits, intellectually as well as emotionally. Some tend to be far more positive than negative, and vice versa. For this analysis, those that are basically positive will receive primary consideration.

Likewise, attachments are a combination of both conscious and non-conscious elements, intellectually as well as emotionally. Since those attachments that are present in the conscious mind, or are capable of being brought to consciousness, can be understood, this study will concentrate on them. However, this does not mean or imply that many significant attachments do not lie beneath the surface of consciousness. They certainly do and they sometimes profoundly affect conscious processes and behavior.

Attachments are very complex and vary in many ways. They can be understood by means of visual depictions as well as verbal descriptions. Therefore, a diagram is provided so that what is explained may be further clarified by what is seen (a way of learning that is important for some readers).

First of all, there are different degrees of intensity. Some are strong while others are weak. That is, there is a stronger attachment to some persons than to others. There are also stronger attachments to certain things, places, events, and intangibles than others.

A university student connects with a particular professor far more than three other professors with whom she is also studying.

Second, attachments to persons are different from other attachments in that an individual participates in an interactive relationship that is not, in most instances, determined strictly by one individual or the other. This is different from those attachments that are determined solely by the individual.

A man has developed a strong attachment to a woman, while she does not have such an attachment to him.

Attachments to persons can be experienced in a variety of ways. An individual may: 1) extend a strong attachment and receive a strong attachment in return; 2) extend a weak one and receive a weak one; 3) extend a strong one, yet only receive a weak one; or 4) extend a weak one, yet receive a strong one. (See diagram on the next page.) An individual may also experience a relationship without an attachment actually taking place. He or she may: 1) extend a strong attachment, but receive none in return; 2) extend none, yet receive a strong one; 3) extend a weak one, but receive none in return; or 4) extend none, and receive only a weak one. (Again, see diagram on the next page.) While each of these categories is illustrative of some possibilities, there are many more that could be identified, particularly if one added some of the complexities that are a part of understanding attachments.

Third, attachments are dynamic in character, becoming stronger and weaker, as well as appearing and disappearing. They do not remain the same over time; however, they generally do not change very rapidly.

A wife grows at a different pace and in a different direction than her husband.

Fourth, attachments are related to each other within the individual, so that a change in one attachment effects a change in another.

A father is torn apart by the serious illness of his three-year-old son and begins to withdraw more and more from his wife.

Fifth, attachments are related to each other outside the individual, so that a change between two attachments effects a change in the individual. (Utilizing the diagram on the next page, additional lines would be drawn between two attachments the individual has—assuming these two attachments are persons.)

A teenager thinks about running away from home because his mother and father, who had verbal arguments with each other

Integrated Visual Summarization

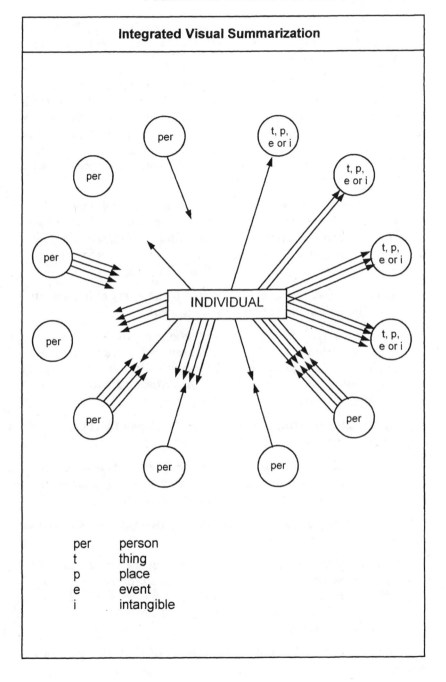

per	person
t	thing
p	place
e	event
i	intangible

in past years, are now yelling and screaming at each other, with his father pushing and slapping his mother in an increasing manner.

Sixth, attachments are also related to other attachments of their own outside the individual, so that a change between those attachments outside the individual effects a change in the attachment the individual has. (Utilizing the diagram again, additional lines would be drawn from an attachment the individual has—assuming it is a person—to other attachments that such a person has.)

A mother loves her son very deeply, but struggles with what she should do now that he is away at college and is developing close relationships with a group of fraternity brothers who, in this particular situation, are more interested in partying, drinking, and sleeping around than studying.

Seventh, attachments are influenced by a variety of forces, some known to the individual and others not known.

A professor is drawn to a student who is so interested in the subject matter of the course, so well prepared, and so articulate in classroom preparation, without realizing that the student is so motivated, in part, because her husband told her she wouldn't succeed.

Eighth, attachments are sometimes developed by choice, while at other times they are developed by circumstance.

A family decides to move to a home in an excellent school district, while another family learns that a very desirable family has just moved into the house next door.

Ninth, attachments are sometimes perceived as one wants them to be.

A father of five school-age children perceives that he has the same degree of attachment to each of his children because he believes this is the way it should be; however, his behavior shows that he actually has a stronger attachment to some of his children than to others.

Tenth, attachments are sometimes perceived as one thinks they are.

A mother thinks she understands the close attachment that she and her 15-year-old daughter have to each other until she overhears her daughter talking with her friends and learns that her daughter doesn't sense hardly any attachment to her at all.

Eleventh, attachments are sometimes perceived as they really are.

A senior citizen describes his relationship with a dear friend to his counselor, who, in turn, meets this dear friend and hears a very similar description of the relationship.

Twelfth, attachments are limited in the amount of emotional capital that is available for investment.

A pastor of a sizeable congregation realizes that she cannot have a close relationship with most members of the church, and that such a relationship is only possible with a relatively limited number of members.

Thirteenth, attachments may be cultivated or neglected.

A husband reflects on his relationship with his wife and decides to find new and creative ways to keep on courting her.

Fourteenth, attachments are the basis for one's meaning in life.

A woman reflects on the persons who are important to her, the things that surround her, the places she loves to visit, the events she enjoys, and the music that stirs her emotions, and she becomes more fully aware of what gives rise to her meaning.

Understanding attachments is an important endeavor before making an attempt to comprehend breaks in attachments. Yet, attachments are far more complex than the way they are set forth in this analysis. Nevertheless, a broad overview such as that which has been presented may provide insights otherwise unrealized, and may also lead to a more in-depth analysis if one chooses to probe their deeper meaning.

EXERCISES FOR READER
AND CAREGIVER

1. Review the integrated visual summarization given in this chapter. Note that lines extend only half the distance when they move toward another person, while they extend the full distance when they connect with a thing, a place, an event, or an intangible.

2. **As a reader** who wants to integrate reading with self-understanding:

    a. Take a sheet of plain paper and diagram your own attachments, putting your name in the center rectangle and names of ten to fifteen of the most important persons, things, places, events, and/or intangibles in the circles that surround the center. Do not be concerned about leaving someone or something out. Record what first comes into your mind.

    b. Connect your name to each of these circles with a single line, extending it halfway toward other persons and the full distance to other attachments.

    c. Add lines to your stronger attachments (two, three, four, or more). Do not add lines from other persons toward you at this time.

    d. After completing the recording, reflect on what you have drawn, recognizing that even though this is a very simplified version of a very complicated life—and therefore to some extent misleading and perhaps even erroneous—there may be insights to be gained in trying to understand your own attachments.

    e. If you want to develop the diagram further, draw lines from other persons to yourself.

    f. Continue your reflection, exploring further insights that may come to mind.

3. **As a caregiver** who wants to understand someone else's life:

    a. Follow the same procedure for that person (on a separate sheet of paper), putting his or her name in the center and carrying on the same process on the basis of how you perceive that person. Keep in mind that this is only your own perception and may be rather inaccurate at some points.

    b. If the relationship is mutual and you want to understand one another's attachments:

1) Invite the other person to follow the same procedure (on separate sheets of paper) that you carried out for yourself.

2) Exchange diagrams and comments in whatever sequence seems most comfortable.

3) Try to understand each other rather than defend the differing perceptions noted of yourselves and each other.

4. **As a caregiver** who wants to help others understand themselves, provide an opportunity for two or more persons to follow the same procedure.

    a. If there is only one person, let him or her reflect on the diagram of his or her life. Raise questions that may lead to a clearer self-perception. Follow other practices that are consistent with appropriate and effective counseling [14, 15].

    b. If there are two persons, assist them in sharing and reflecting on the diagrams of their own attachments.

    c. If there is a group of persons, assist them in the same manner, dividing the group, if it is large, into small groups in order for sharing and reflection to take place by those who are willing to reveal themselves in this manner.

5. Find other ways to adapt these exercises in creative and effective ways.

REFERENCES AND NOTES

1. J. Bowlby, *Loss: Sadness and Depression,* Basic Books, London, 1980.
2. J. Bowlby, *The Making and Breaking of Affectional Bonds,* Tavistock, London, 1979, particularly pp. 129-133, where the author delineates his understanding of proximity.
3. M. S. Ainsworth, M. C. Blehar, E. Waters, and S. Wall, *Patterns of Attachment: A Psychological Study of the Strange Situation,* Lawrence Erlbaum Associates, Hillsdale, New Jersey, 1978.
4. M. S. Ainsworth, Attachments and Other Affectional Bonds, in *Attachments Across the Life Cycle,* C. M. Parkes, J. Stevenson, and P. Marris (eds.), Routledge, London, 1991.
5. C. M. Parkes and J. Stevenson-Hinde (eds.), *The Place of Attachment in Human Behavior,* Tavistock, London, 1982.
6. C. M. Parkes, J. Stevenson-Hinde, and P. Marris (eds.), *Attachment Across the Life Cycle,* Routledge, London, 1991. For a historical survey and extensive bibliography, see pp. 9-32.

7. S. Goldberg, R. Muir, and J. Kerr, *Attachment Theory: Social, Developmental, and Clinical Perspectives,* Analytic Press, Hillsdale, New Jersey, 1995.
8. J. Cassidy and P. Shaver, *Handbook of Attachment: Theory, Research, and Clinical Applications,* Guilford, New York, 1999.
9. For a review of such resources, see *Attachment Resources Catalog 2001-2002,* Mental Health Resources, Saugerties, New York, 2001.
10. *Journal of the American Psychoanalytical Association,* 48:4, 2000. For an overview of attachment theory, see M. Main, The Organized Categories of Infant, Child, and Adult Attachment: Flexible vs. Inflexible Attention Under Attachment-Related Stress, pp. 1055-1096. See also A. Slade, The Development and Organization of Attachment: Implications for Psychoanalysis, pp. 1147-1174.
11. A. Richards and P. Tyson, Psychoanalysis, Development and the Life Cycle, *Journal of the American Psychoanalytical Association,* 48:4, 2000.
12. P. Fonagy, *Attachment Theory and Psychoanalysis,* Other, New York, 2001. See also the comprehensive listing of references, pp. 193-246.
13. J. Holmes, *The Search for the Secure Base: Attachment Theory and Psychotherapy,* Taylor & Francis, Philadelphia, 2001.
14. W. Worden, *Grief Counseling and Grief Therapy: A Handbook for the Mental Health Practitioner* (3rd Edition), Springer, New York, 2002.
15. D. Capps, *Giving Counsel: A Minister's Guidebook,* Chalice, St. Louis, 2001.

CHAPTER 2

Loss as a Break in an Attachment

Attachments do not remain constant. Sometimes they become stronger; sometimes they become weaker; sometimes they break.

All human beings who have reached the age of accountability experience breaks in attachments. For most it either has included, or eventually will include, breaks in affectional bonds. A parent may move out, or get a divorce. A sibling may develop close relationships outside the family, or go away to school. A close friend may choose to spend time with others, or relocate to another part of the country. Or any one of these bonds may break because a death has taken place.

However, for some persons there will not be the experience of dealing with breaks in affectional bonds, because they have never developed such attachments of their own. Carole McKelvey and her colleagues describe this phenomenon in a book written in conjunction with The Attachment Center at Evergreen, Colorado, *Give Them Roots, Then Let Them Fly: Understanding Attachment Therapy* [1].

In this volume, the authors delineate reactive attachment disorders as well as therapeutic treatments, focusing on children who do not form an affectional bond with their birth mother, foster mother, adoptive mother, or other primary caregiver such as their father or other surrogate parent. As a result, these children do not experience trust at a deep and significant level, and therefore cannot trust another person to care for them. A further result is that they do not learn to care for others and consequently have little or no conscience regarding how they treat others. They have never become attached at any significant level of depth. They can easily become candidates not only for juvenile delinquency, but also for antisocial personality disorders throughout their adult lives.

Developing one or more meaningful affectional bonds during infancy and childhood is so important to finding a fulfilled life. Yet it is those who develop such bonds who also experience the pain that comes when a break takes place. Those who have an attachment disorder do not feel the pain of separation when it occurs because there is no affectional bond that has been broken. Oftentimes they are solitary individuals who have never really connected with others [2, pp. 58-103].

On the other hand, for those who have developed attachments and affectional bonds in their early years, there are breaks that emerge throughout life. They most often can be characterized as losses. So common are they that it is not an overstatement to say, *to live is to experience loss.*

The subject of loss, which comprises the theme of this chapter, has increasingly become a subject of investigation. John Harvey has edited a volume, *Perspectives on Loss: A Sourcebook,* that summarizes studies that have been carried out and explores the case for a psychology of loss [3]. Whether loss studies will become a separate and identifiable field of scholarship remains to be seen.

More recently, John Harvey authored a volume, *Perspectives on Loss and Trauma: Assaults on the Self* [4]. In it he focuses on five principles and applies them to a variety of loss experiences. The first four indicate that major losses are relative, have cumulative effects, contribute to new aspects of our identity, and involve adaptations related to our sense of control. The fifth principle identifies coping strategies for dealing with loss, including "working on the meanings of the losses" and "learning how to give back to others based on our lessons of loss" [4, p. 30]. This final principle is stated in a variety of ways in his work, as will also be done in this volume.

The subject of loss is also explored in the comprehensive volume by Lynne DeSpelder and Albert Strickland, *The Last Dance: Encountering Death and Dying,* a book that has already undergone seven editions [5]. The chapter in which this occurs is significant because it is set in a very broad context of social as well as personal perspectives [5, pp. 267-307].

Loss begins with the individual who experiences a break in an attachment and, if it is a significant break, loses part of one's self.

Even if the individual does not understand this to be the case, it nevertheless does take place. Colin Murray Parkes, as well as many others, speaks of this in terms of giving up an old identity and gaining a new one [6, pp. 89-106]. Such an experience is at the core of what makes a significant break so consequential.

A break involves some degree of process, even if that process is brief. For example, even in the short duration of time that it takes for a white cue ball to strike the leading ball in the pyramidal arrangement of fifteen colored balls set up on a billiard table, there is some process involved. The player with the cue stick lines up the shot. Aim is taken and the cue ball is firmly struck. The leading ball is hit and—if it is a good shot—all fifteen balls scatter on the table in a random pattern. A series of actions have occurred. A result has been achieved, though its implications have not yet been realized.

More often, a break in an attachment takes place in the context of a process that continues for some period of time. An attachment becomes threatened, even before it actually occurs. Then it begins to weaken and a break begins. It then goes through further weakening and the break becomes more obvious. Finally, the attachment is severed and the break actually takes place. Each of these developments may be seen, for example, in a relationship between two individuals. Yet the progression will not ordinarily be in such a linear and sequential progression. It will be much more random and unpredictable.

A break takes place in a variety of ways. It may come about very suddenly, like an egg that is firmly cracked open. It may begin gradually, like a runner in a marathon race. It may begin indecisively, like a car caught in heavy traffic. It may begin unnoticeably, like a pan heating water. It may begin and then disappear, like a baseball batter who checks his swing. It may be anticipated, but not begin, like a storm that is announced, but doesn't arrive.

A break may—and often will—include some combination of these possibilities. This is particularly the case when a break in an attachment has not yet actually occurred. In addition, a break may not eventuate in a total severing of the attachment, even though the attachment may become substantially changed.

Life is filled with many variations of breaks. In order to categorize them in a way that is broad in scope, yet specific in function, this analysis utilizes a method of correlation between attachments and breaks (i.e., the same overall categories being used in this chapter as were used in chapter one).

PERSONS

An unlimited number of intrapsychic phenomena could be included in this category. Some examples are: loss of self-esteem, change in lifestyle, loss of purpose, loss of identity, loss of an ability to cope, passage of a stage, loss of youth, a new image, an unfulfilled expectation, or loss of security.

RELATIONSHIP WITH OTHERS

Since most affectional bonds that individuals experience take place within the context of a family (whether understood in the traditional sense of a man, a woman, and their offspring, or in some other configuration that constitutes a grouping of persons in their primary relationships), the examples that follow utilize that frame of reference.

A primary person in the family is one's *spouse* (however that term is defined). Common breaks in attachments are: growth at a different pace, growth in a different direction, being away from home, living in another location, separation in more formalized ways, divorce, or the most difficult of all, death.

Another primary group is *children*. Some examples for one or both parents are: a pregnancy, an unwanted pregnancy, a miscarriage, an abortion, the birth of a child, the birth of an unhealthy child, a new venture, going to school, becoming a teenager, graduation from school, leaving home, marriage, or death. Such examples are also applicable to sibling relationships.

Still another group is *parents*. Examples include the aging process, illnesses of various kinds, senility, loss of independence, breaking up housekeeping, entering a senior citizen's residence, loss of functions, skills, and/or capacities, or death.

Included in each of these three groupings are not only the individuals who are involved, but also the *family systems* of which they are a part. The influence of the system on the individual is very significant in a number of ways, including the way it has developed, the structure that has emerged, the social context of which it is a part, the religious norms and values that it embraces or rejects, and the dynamics that it manifests. Likewise, the influence of the individual—as a differentiated self—on the system is also very significant. Furthermore, the family system is also important for a caregiver to understand when he or she interacts with one or more individuals within it, whether that caregiver is a family friend, a member of the clergy, a social worker, or a counselor [7-13]. For an individual who experiences a significant break in an attachment is part of a system of relationships, however that system is defined.

Even beyond these groupings, and their multiple personal and systemic interactions, there are the *other relationships* that an individual has in social settings and professional contexts. Included in these relationships there are breaks in attachments that emerge. These include loss of communication, loss of respect for someone, a broken friendship, not being accepted, loss of an important person, loss of a lover, or, once again, death. And for some, the loss of God, particularly if one experiences God as a personal being (while defining God as far more than such a being).

THINGS

Specific items that might be lost are too numerous to identify. However, a few types of material possessions are: loss of an object of importance, loss of a personal possession, destruction of one's living quarters, loss of a pet (though for many far more than a "thing"), a significant decrease in one's investment portfolio, a bankruptcy, loss of financial security, or a change in standard of living.

PLACES

Locations to which one has become attached can also be experienced as a break. Examples include a move away from home, a transfer to a new community, a change in a neighborhood, loss of familiar surroundings, going to the hospital, going to jail, loss of a landmark, or loss of one's environment or part of the very environment itself.

EVENTS

Actual occurrences that constitute a break in an attachment sometimes take place on a personal level. Examples include loss of health, loss of a bodily organ, loss of a bodily function, a physical hardship, a job transfer, a job promotion, being bypassed for a promotion, a job demotion, loss of employment, change of vocation, or retirement.

Other breaks in attachments are more societal. Examples are: loss of a tradition, loss of a freedom, shift in mores, change in leadership, new minister/priest/rabbi/imam, revision in ecclesiastical practice, loss of a cause, loss of a political election, or loss of an athletic event.

INTANGIBLES

Elusive matters to which individuals become attached can also be broken. Examples include loss of a dream or a vision, a change in ideas, a shift in values, an environment with limited art forms, an absence of music, or an atmosphere of apprehension/distrust/fear.

A break in an attachment—a loss—is initiated in a variety of ways. More often than not, it comes about as a result of chance. In other words, *stuff happens*. The causal factor is either not known or it is a mixture of multiple forces that are so complex that a clear delineation of causality is not possible, at least not in a manner that is reliable and verifiable. A miscarriage occurs, a child gets sick, a truck hits a spouse, a parent becomes senile, a close friend dies, an investment plummets dramatically, a landmark is destroyed, a job is terminated, a vision is lost. *Stuff happens*.

At other times a break occurs as a result of choice. An individual chooses to move to a new community. A man decides to leave his wife. A woman chooses to have an abortion. A child commits suicide. A parent decides to enter a senior citizens' residence. A friend breaks up a relationship. An older woman sells her car. An older man moves in with his children. An individual decides to retire. Another gives up a dream.

Actual breaks in attachments occur—at least to some extent—by chance. And actual breaks take place—at least to some extent— by choice. The extent to which each is involved is often difficult to discern. One's upbringing may be such that there is no real choice possible. Or, one's resources may be so limited that a particular option is almost a foregone conclusion. Or, one's circumstances may be so prescribed that making a decision has not even been considered.

A break in an attachment is often not desirable. This is due, primarily, to the fact that the attachment is desirable. When a person is ill, or in an accident, or grows old and is unable to walk, the break is, obviously, undesirable.

Sometimes, however, a break is desirable. When a child grows up, a break with childhood is perceived as a positive development. When a teenager finds a more meaningful way to state an idea, a break with a simplistic expression is considered a development in maturity. When an adult breaks an attachment that is basically negative in character, such as alcoholism or drug addiction, a break is understood as a wholesome occurrence.

There are other times when a break may or may not be desirable. When an individual changes her or his job, there might be great joy or considerable consternation. If the job is a promotion with a significantly higher salary, additional flexibility of schedule, and increased opportunity to make a real difference in the life of the organization, the change is welcomed and celebrated. If the job is a demotion due to the corporation downsizing and the new position being lower in salary, more rigid in schedule, and very little opportunity to make a significant contribution, the shift in employment is greeted with frustration and disdain.

There are still other times when a break in an attachment is both desirable and undesirable, especially when it involves more than one person. When a family moves across the country to a new community because a father has been transferred by the company and given a very lucrative promotion, there may be a daughter who is a debate team captain entering her junior year in high school in a couple of months, a son who is an emerging track star beginning eighth grade, and a mother who feels the anguish of separation from her colleagues at work as well as her many friends with whom she feels such a strong attachment.

Furthermore, a break in an attachment is, at times, also necessary. Judith Viorst, in her book *Necessary Losses: The Loves, Illusions, Dependencies, and Impossible Expectations That All of Us Have to Give Up in Order to Grow,* delineates a point of view that shows how our losses are linked to our growth [14]. "Our losses," she says, "include not only our separation and departures from those we love, but our conscious and unconscious losses of romantic dreams, impossible expectations, illusions of freedom and power, illusions of safety—and the loss of our own younger self, the self that thought it always would be unwrinkled and invulnerable and immortal" [14, pp. 15-16]. These, and others like them, are lifelong losses as well as necessary losses. They are inescapable, not only as a part of the fabric of life, but also as essential ingredients to growth.

Still further, a break is sometimes permanent and irrevocable, while at other times it is temporary and changeable. When a person loses a limb, an eye, or certain other parts of the body, the loss is final. When a person fractures a bone, injures an eye or another part of the body, the loss is usually limited in time. So is also the case with certain losses of bodily functions. Some are permanent while others are temporary. And, of course, the most irrevocable of all is the experience of death, regardless of what claims some individuals attempt to assert regarding experiences that involve death and a return to life.

Finally, a break in an attachment—a loss—may also be seen from a variety of perspectives. Kenneth Mitchell and Herbert Anderson speak about the experience of "leaving" and "being left" [15, pp. 50-51]. They point out that a loss is experienced differently by the one who leaves and the one who is left. The former is thought of as one who chooses an action, while the latter is the one who is the recipient of the action. When a daughter or a son leaves home, the other members of the family are left with one person less. What the daughter or son loses is somewhat different from what the rest of the family loses.

Throughout one's life, breaks in attachments occur—again, and again, and again. No one is exempt. In other words, to live is to experience loss. Yet the whole crux of the matter depends on how one responds—a subject that will be the focus of the chapters that follow.

EXERCISES FOR READER
AND CAREGIVER

1. Review the exercise that you completed at the end of Chapter 1 in order to be reminded of your attachments (as you perceived them at the time you completed the exercise, realizing that if you did the exercise again—without looking at what you previously recorded—the results would probably be somewhat different).

2. **As a reader** who wants to integrate reading with self-understanding:

    a. Take a sheet of paper and make a list of the breaks in attachments (i.e., losses) you have experienced in the past. Do not try to be inclusive of all losses. Name only those that easily come to mind. Then, reflect on what you have recorded, and note which one seems to be your greatest loss. Try to understand what led you to such a conclusion.

b. Consider additional reflection, perhaps with another person who is willing to listen and hear what you are feeling as well as what you are thinking.

3. **As a caregiver** who wants to understand someone else's life:

a. Follow the same procedure for that person (on a separate sheet of paper), making a list of his or her breaks in attachments (past, present, near future) on the basis of how you perceive that person. Remember to proceed with caution since this exercise oversimplifies to a considerable extent.

b. If the relationship is mutual and you want to understand one another's breaks in attachments:

1) Invite the other person to follow the same procedure (on separate sheets of paper) that you carried out for yourself.

2) Exchange lists and comments in whatever sequence seems most comfortable.

3) Try to understand each other's breaks in attachments, both intellectually and emotionally.

4. **As a caregiver** who wants to help others understand themselves, provide an opportunity for two or more persons to follow the same procedure. Utilize the guidelines given in the exercise at the end of Chapter 1.

5. Find other ways to adapt these exercises. For example, record breaks in attachments that have occurred in the past in chronological order. Or, review breaks that occurred during certain ages (infancy, childhood, adolescence, etc.). Or, after listing past breaks, reflect on which ones were consequential over a short period of time and which ones continued for a long time. Or, work out other creative and effective adaptations.

REFERENCES AND NOTES

1. C. A. McKelvey (ed.), *Give Them Roots, Then Let Them Fly: Understanding Attachment Therapy*, Morris, Philadelphia, 1995.

2. K. Magid and C. A. McKelvey, *High Risk: Children Without a Conscience*, Bantam, New York, 1987.

3. J. H. Harvey (ed.), *Perspectives on Loss: A Sourcebook*, Brunner/Mazel, Philadelphia, Pennsylvania, 1998. Note especially Chapter 1 by E. Miller

and J. Omarzu; Chapter 24 by J. H. Harvey and A. Weber; and Chapter 25 by R. Neimeyer.

4. J. H. Harvey, *Perspectives on Loss and Trauma: Assaults on the Self,* Sage, Thousand Oaks, California, 2002.

5. L. A. DeSpelder and A. L. Strickland, *The Last Dance: Encountering Death and Dying,* McGraw-Hill, New York, 2005.

6. C. M. Parkes, *Bereavement: Studies of Grief in Adult Life* (3rd Edition), International Universities, Madison, 1998.

7. J. Winchester Nadeau, *Families Making Sense of Death,* Sage, Thousand Oaks, California, 1998.

8. E. Rosen, *Families Facing Death: A Guide for Healthcare Professionals and Volunteers* (Rev. Edition), Jossey-Bass, San Francisco, 1998.

9. E. Shapiro, *Grief as a Family Process: A Developmental Approach to Clinical Practice,* Guilford, New York, 1994.

10. F. Walsh and M. McGoldrick (eds.), *Living Beyond Loss: Death in the Family,* W. W. Norton, New York, 1991.

11. B. Carter and M. McGoldrick, *The Changing Family Life Cycle: A Framework for Family Therapy* (2nd Edition), Gardner, New York, 1988.

12. C. Hollingsworth and R. Pasnau, *The Family in Mourning: A Guide for Health Professionals,* Grune and Stratton, New York, 1977.

13. J. W. Worden, *Grief Counseling and Grief Therapy: A Handbook for the Mental Health Practitioner* (3rd Edition), pp. 149-172, Springer, New York, 2002.

14. J. Viorst, *Necessary Losses: The Loves, Illusions, Dependencies, and Impossible Expectations That All of Us Have to Give Up in Order to Grow,* Simon and Schuster, New York, 1986.

15. K. Mitchell and H. Anderson, *All Our Losses, All Our Griefs: Resources for Pastoral Care,* Westminster, Philadelphia, 1983.

CHAPTER 3

Responding to a Break

Having recognized that breaks occur, this chapter will focus on the thesis of this book, namely, the need to respond. In its most succinct form it can be stated in two sentences:

To live is to experience loss.
To survive is to learn how to respond [1].

The first sentence affirms that every person experiences breaks in attachments. The second sets forth the crux of this volume, namely, that survival is dependent upon a person learning how to respond, especially if that survival is permeated by meaning that is deep, significant, and ongoing. It will be dealt with, not only in this chapter, but in those that follow as well.

One of the most prominent proponents of the assumption underlying this perspective is Viktor Frankl. In his book, *Man's Search for Meaning,* first published in German in 1946 [2], he describes his experiences during the time he spent in a concentration camp during the Second World War (part one), and then analyzes his experiences and sets forth the basic concepts of logotherapy (part two). Subsequent revisions have been made and published in a variety of formats [3].

At the core of Frankl's writing is his formulation of logotherapy, a school of psychotherapy that focuses on the will to meaning rather than the will to pleasure (Freud) or the will to power (Adler). Accordingly, it asserts that meaning in life is found in three different ways [1, p. 133]. The first is by creating a work or doing a deed. The second is by experiencing something such as truth, beauty, goodness, or another human being in love.

The third is by the attitude a person takes toward unavoidable suffering.

Throughout these ways there is a focus on the future rather than the past, that is, on the meaning to be found by the individual in his or her response to the present. For Frankl, this response is to something or someone outside of oneself. Thus, he calls it self-transcendence rather than self-actualization, with self-actualization only possible as a side effect of self-transcendence. A similar approach is utilized by Ashley Prend in her volume *Transcending Loss: Understanding the Lifelong Impact of Grief and How to Make It Meaningful* [4].

Central to Frankl's thesis is the freedom that every functioning human being has to respond to his or her own situation—whatever that situation may be. It is not freedom from any particular condition, but a freedom to take a stand in response to a condition, however limited the residue of freedom may be. Even in neurotic and psychotic cases, an individual has at the core of his or her personality some degree of freedom to respond. The usefulness of an individual may be gone, but not his or her dignity [1, p. 156].

Nevertheless, freedom can degenerate into arbitrariness if it is not lived in terms of responsibleness. In the words of Frankl, "logotherapy sees in responsibleness the very essence of human existence" [1, p. 131]. Therefore he can formulate a categorical imperative for logotherapy: "Live as if you were living already for the second time and as if you had acted the first time as wrongly as you are about to act now!" [1, p. 132].

Such freedom can also be identified and affirmed in difficult situations other than a concentration camp. For example, individuals who are seriously ill—even terminally ill—can exercise some degree of freedom as they respond to their particular situation, even if that freedom is quite limited. Furthermore, if they exercise this freedom in a responsible manner, they can find meaning in the midst of profound anguish and pain.

When individuals experience a loss, they have freedom to respond, even when that freedom is very small. They may not realize that they have this freedom. As a result, they may not believe that they have any freedom at all. However, their lack of awareness and/or their lack of belief do not mean they are without freedom.

Individuals *can* choose to respond, though they may need a caregiver to help them come to this realization. And they can do this over a period of time, not only at one particular time. In other words, they can share in a process of responding. Although this process is unique to each individual, there are some patterns that do emerge.

This chapter will look at an overview of such a process. Chapters 4 and 5 will analyze that process in terms of patterns that emerge before a break in an attachment has taken place and after such a break has occurred. Chapter 6 will reexamine what has been analyzed and will then put it together as a synthesis. A diagram will be utilized in each of these chapters to illustrate visually what is stated verbally.

That general patterns do emerge in responses individuals make to loss experiences is accepted by many, even when those patterns are identified in various ways. However, that specific stages take place—ones that are rigidly defined, sequentially fixed, and prescriptively advocated—is widely rejected. Individuals respond in particular ways. Nevertheless, there are some similarities that often emerge.

In this examination, the term *phases* will be used to identify those broad similarities that emerge in an unfolding pattern of response [5-7]. However, the phases that are identified will not be rigidly defined, will not be sequentially fixed, and will not be prescriptively advocated. They will be set forth in a manner that is conditional, flexible, and descriptive.

This latter category is very crucial in a study such as this one. Persons who read about a phase that is set forth in a descriptive manner may, without even realizing it, interpret the phase in a prescriptive manner. That is, they may think this is how they, or someone they are thinking about, should respond. Furthermore, if they do reflect in this way, they may also think something is not right if they do not respond in this way.

Phases utilized in this analysis are set forth as descriptive explanations of what *often* happens to *a number* of people who respond to a break in an attachment—a loss. Such phases do not *always* occur in *all* people.

The overview of the process that is set forth in the diagram on the next page has four components implicit in its structure. First, there is a sequential movement—overall—from left to right. Second, there is an event given in the vertical column in the center, namely, the identification of *a break in that to which one is attached*. Third, there are phases prior to the break and phases after the break.

Overview of the Process		
INDIVIDUAL — moving through phases →	break in that to	— moving through phases →
OTHERS — moving through phases → (family) — moving through phases → (friends) — moving through phases → (caregivers)	which one is attached	— moving through phases → (family) — moving through phases → (friends) — moving through phases → (caregivers)

Fourth, there is the top half for the *individual* and the bottom half for *others* (with three sets of horizontal lines to refer to family, friends, and caregivers) [8].

The diagram requires some explanation for its meaning to be clear. The sequential movement from left to right that represents the experience of an individual is never along a straight line. It is not even always in a sequential movement from left to right. It meanders in a variety of directions, sometimes repetitively, sometimes in a cyclical or spiral pattern. Yet its overall pattern— when seen over a period of time—does move ahead if the response of an individual is a reasonably healthy one.

The event that is identified as a break in an attachment is not always an occurrence at one point in time. A break, as we have already noted in Chapter 2, may begin gradually, indecisively, or unnoticeably; may begin and disappear; may be anticipated, yet not begin.

Oftentimes there are phases that take place prior to a break in an attachment, except when the break is sudden and unexpected. There are also phases that take place after a break. These phases on either side of the break are not the same, even though there is a considerable amount of similarity.

Finally, there is the experience of the *individual* in relation to his or her break in an attachment as well as the experiences of *others* (family, friends, caregivers, etc.), particularly as they attempt to relate to the individual who is dealing with his or her break. As the individual moves through phases, the others are also moving through phases, sometimes at a similar pace to that of the individual, sometimes at a different pace, and oftentimes some of each. In fact, there are usually a number of others relating to the individual, each of whom is moving at his or her own pace, in his or her own manner, and within his or her network of relationships. The result is often a complex series of dynamics that needs very insightful discernment and very careful interaction.

When the break in an attachment is a death, the upper right-hand quadrant becomes an unknown. Beliefs about the experience of the individual who has died may be affirmed; however, knowledge about any actual experience is beyond the capacity of empirical verification. Therefore, phases cannot be meaningfully explored under such circumstances.

Nevertheless, phases that others often go through can be described. This is precisely where research regarding phases began, namely, in the lower right-hand quadrant of the diagram. One of the earliest to identify "a definite syndrome" in what persons experience following the death of a loved one, and to publish his findings to a broad audience in 1944, was Erich Lindemann in his well-known article, "Symptomatology and Management of Acute Grief" [9]. In it he describes five symptoms he identified in the bereaved: somatic distress, preoccupation with the image of the deceased, guilt, hostile reactions, and loss of patterns of conduct. He also delineates three tasks that are carried out in what he calls "grief work," namely, emancipation from the bondage to the deceased, readjustment to the environment in which the deceased is missing, and the formation of new relationships [9, p. 170].

Many others built upon, or deviated from, this analysis in the decades that followed, focusing their attention primarily on the lower, right-hand quadrant of the diagram. The most prominent of these are summarized by Therese Rando in her historical review in *Treatment of Complicated Mourning* [6, pp. 79-147].

In the midst of these analyses of experiences that persons go through after a break in an attachment—in most instances a death—Elisabeth Kübler-Ross emerged on the scene as a very significant figure. Her first notable publication, *On Death and Dying* in 1969 [10], her sequel to this volume, *Questions and Answers on Death and Dying* in 1974 [11], and numerous interviews, articles, and subsequent publications led her to a position of prominence in a movement that would become known across the country.

The work of Kübler-Ross focused in the upper left-hand quadrant of the diagram as she carried on her investigation to learn from dying patients what they were going through. This was a dramatic shift from what had been learned about the grieving process *after* a death had taken place. It focused on what an individual was experiencing *before* his or her death actually occurred.

Furthermore, Kübler-Ross' investigation dealt primarily with the individual's experience of his or her own impending death, and not upon what others were going through as they responded to someone else's anticipated death. Thus, the shift was both from the right side to the left side of the diagram and from the lower to the upper. In other words, it went from the lower right-hand quadrant to the upper left-hand quadrant.

As her writing developed, Kübler-Ross also went on to include what others were experiencing as they related to the individual who was dying; that is, those in the lower left-hand quadrant of the diagram. This included physicians, nurses, and other caregivers as well as family members and friends.

The popularity of her work was not only because of this shift in focus, but also because individuals were being asked to look at their own deaths in a way that was more direct and more explicit than ever before in American culture. No longer was the denial of death an easy stance to maintain. The subject of death was out in the open in the 1970s and more and more people were talking about it. It was no longer a taboo. It was the new subject for college courses and for all sorts of educational endeavors [12].

Some authors describe the process of grieving without differentiating whether the experience is before a break in an attachment has taken place, or after such a break. Thomas Attig, for example, groups Kübler-Ross together with Lindemann, Bowlby, Engel, and Parkes in his commentary on stages in the grieving process [13, p. 42]. Similarly, Robert Neimeyer names the stages identified by Kübler-Ross prior to a death, though the framework of his discussion is bereavement following a death [14, p. 264].

Having an understanding in mind and visualizing that conceptualization in the form of a diagram is, however, not sufficient. An individual, and those to whom he or she relates, needs to move through a process. First, they need to determine where they are:

A man who is undergoing chemotherapy for a rapidly advancing cancer needs to be aware of where he is in the upper left-hand quadrant (as well as where his wife is in the lower left-hand quadrant).

A wife who is dealing with this husband who is dying of cancer needs to be aware of where he is in the upper left-hand quadrant (as well as where she is in the lower left-hand quadrant).

A pastor who has this husband and wife as parishioners needs to be aware of where the husband is, and where the wife is (as well as where he himself is in the lower left-hand quadrant).

Second, each of these individuals needs to act on the basis of what each of them understands, and move through phases of a process while, at the same time, assisting others as they also move through phases. While writers such as Camille Wortman and Roxane Silver claim that individuals do not need to "work through" a process [15], a number of proponents in the field do not concur with such an interpretation, if it is understood that persons can grieve strictly by means of intellectual processing.

In addition to the individual dealing with his or her own experience, he or she may shift roles and become one of the others relating to a different individual, whether the role is as a family member or some other type of caregiver.

> *A man who is himself dying of cancer is relating to his roommate who has just lost a limb and is trying to assist him in his grief (thereby functioning in the lower left-hand quadrant).*

Still further, one may become one of the others relating, not to a different individual, but to one or more of the others who are relating to the individual, whether the role is from one family member to another or from a caregiver to a friend of the family.

> *This same man is also relating to his roommate's friend and is trying to assist her in her grief (thereby functioning, once again, in the lower left-hand quadrant).*

An individual may also view the process and see himself or herself in more than one place at the same time as he or she analyzes more than one break in an attachment.

> *This same man who is dying of cancer is also dealing with the loss of a dog that was recently run over by a truck outside his home (thereby functioning in the upper left-hand quadrant and the lower right-hand quadrant).*

In other words, the framework of the process can be used in a variety of ways in a given situation as well as in a variety of circumstances.

Before turning to an analysis of phases that often take place before and after a break in an attachment, there are three categories of interpretation that need to be clarified. One is the meaning and usage of *certain terms*. A second is the meaning and functioning of *emotional processing*. A third is the meaning and functioning of *intellectual processing*.

Certain terms have already been defined and utilized, words such as *attachment, break,* and *loss*. Others need further clarification before they are utilized in subsequent chapters, particularly *grief, mourning,* and *bereavement*. Even though they are interchangeable in certain contexts, they will be more useful if they are, at least in part, distinguished from one another.

Grief is a term that refers to a reaction to a break in an attachment—to a loss—but not any loss. The attachment must be substantial and significant for grief to be experienced. The dropping of a coin when taking change out of one's purse does not usually produce grief. The loss of one's purse usually does, especially—for example—if it was stolen while in another country and contained a passport, a return airline ticket, considerable cash, multiple credit cards, and other crucial items of identification.

Furthermore, grief is not a momentary matter. It is a process. It focuses, on the one hand, in anguish and sorrow, and, on the other, in finding meaning in the midst of such pain. Its intensity is determined by the loss—its significance, its nature, and its permanence. As difficult as it is to deal with a stolen purse while overseas, it doesn't begin to compare with the depth of excruciating pain that parents experience when their child is killed.

Grief is utilized by Rando as a term that refers to a process of reactions to loss. She describes four ways in which this occurs: "*psychologically* (through affects, cognitions, perceptions, attitudes, and philosophy/spirituality), *behaviorally* (through personal action, conduct, or demeanor), *socially* (through reactions to and interactions with others), and *physically* (through bodily symptoms and physical health)" [6, p. 22]. These categories are modified by Roslyn Karaban, in *Complicated Losses, Difficult Deaths,* who includes both the psychological and the physical, combines the social and behavioral into one category, and separates out the spiritual as a category by itself [16, pp. 1-4]. This allows her to deal with the spiritual dimensions of grief in a more significant manner.

Mourning is a term that deals with the expression of grief. It can be used to designate the personal, and oftentimes private, expressions of grief, though it is more often utilized to refer to the expression of public grief, especially in the use of connectional outward signs of grief for the dead, whether those signs are shown in articles of clothing worn, in places visited, in acts carried out, or in particular time periods governing certain patterns of behavior.

Rando gives a particular meaning to the term mourning that includes "actions undertaken to cope with, adapt suitably to, and accommodate that loss and its ramifications" [8, p. 4]. She limits the definition of grief to "reactions to the perceptions of loss" [8, p. 4]. While such a distinction may be made, it is by no means necessary. The denotation of these two terms does not call for it. Therefore, these meanings will not be strictly followed in this analysis.

Bereavement is a term that has its root meaning in deprivation. It implies, according to Collin Murray Parkes, "the absence of a necessary person or thing as opposed to loss of that person or thing" [5, p. 9]. An individual who is experiencing grief is, therefore, responding to both loss and deprivation. As grief is the response to loss, loneliness is the response to deprivation.

In this analysis the term *grief* will be understood and utilized as a process that describes both the experience of anguish and sorrow and the experience of meaning making in response to a loss (the inner circle). Mourning will also be utilized as the expression of grief, particularly when it is public (the outer circle). The term bereavement will be limited to references pertaining to deprivation.

A second category of interpretation that will be utilized in subsequent chapters is the understanding and functioning of *emotional processing*. The understanding is not difficult to grasp, but the functioning needs some elaboration. For it is a process that begins at the time one learns of a break that may be coming, or at the time when a break has already occurred. Although present earlier in the process, it does not come into focus until there is a realization of what may be happening, or has already happened.

A complete emotional release does not usually take place in any final manner. However, through a period of processing feelings—often a very long period of time—an individual can come to a substantial emotional release. That is, he or she can come to the point of not living with grief, in response to a particular loss, on a constant basis. This does not mean that grief does not continue; it only means that grief can come and go. Yet, when it comes, it can still be very intense, even though it often does not last for as long a period of time as it once did.

In order to achieve a substantial emotional release, an individual—at least in most situations—needs to carry out the following: a) get in touch with his or her own feelings; b) understand what they are; c) own them; and d) express them in ways that are consistent with one's own personality, conducive to one's own growth, not harmful to someone else's growth, and acceptable to his or her social environment (unless, for example, one is protesting his or her situation and is willing to accept the consequences for such actions). These are not simple or easy steps to carry out. They often take considerable work over a significant period of time.

Feelings are expressed in many ways. Sometimes words are used. Sometimes actions. Sometimes a combination of the two. And oftentimes, when intense feelings regarding a break in an attachment surface, tears emerge and flow, and flow. And these tears are very significant in the grieving process for a high percentage of individuals, men as well as women.

It is important to understand that a feeling is OK to have, regardless of what it is. Feeling joy is OK; so is feeling sorrow. Feeling pleasure is OK; so is feeling anger. Feeling honor is OK; so is feeling shame. Feelings simply *are*!

Furthermore, a feeling ought not to be denied on the basis of what someone else says. "Oh, don't feel like that" is heard over and over again. It gives the implicit message that the feeling is not right to have. It also often creates another feeling, namely, guilt. As a result, the individual who experiences a particular feeling is encouraged to deny it and then feel guilty for having it in the first place.

A third category that will also be utilized in subsequent chapters is the understanding and functioning of *intellectual processing*. The initial understanding is not difficult to grasp. The mind needs to work through what has happened. However, the processing is far more than a realization of what has taken place. And it comes into focus after that realization has emerged.

As one works through feelings in the phase of emotional processing, one also needs to make sense of what has taken place, what is currently taking place, and what may take place. This is the phase of intellectual processing. It develops as a *modification* of meaning when the break is approaching, but has not yet happened. That is, meaning is often altered or adjusted, rather that recreated [17]. However, when the break has already happened, it develops as a *reconstruction* of meaning.

Neimeyer has edited a volume that broadens the thesis set forth in his earlier work, *Lessons of Loss: A Guide to Coping* [18]. It is entitled *Meaning Reconstruction and the Experience of Loss.*

In this book, he and a number of others set forth the critical importance of meaning reconstruction in response to a loss that has already taken place. In his own article, "The Language of Loss: Grief Therapy as a Process of Meaning Reconstruction" [14, pp. 261-292], he explicitly identifies a framework of understanding and illustrates its utilization in an actual therapy session, as he draws upon a constructivist approach to psychology. In doing so, he presents significant loss as "a challenge to one's sense of narrative coherence as well as to the sense of identity for which they were an important source of validation" [14, p. 263].

For Attig [13, pp. 3-24], as well as Neimeyer, stories are a primary means through which an individual shares his or her personal narrative. In the event of a loss, the narrative is interrupted—mildly, substantially, or devastatingly. Yet the individual goes on living and must face the need of incorporating the experience of the loss in his or her personal narrative in a way that *modifies* or *reconstructs* it in a meaningful way.

The emotional processing is of particular importance to the griever who tends to be more intuitive, while the intellectual processing is of particular significance to the griever who leans more toward an instrumental expression. Terry Martin and Kenneth Doka contrast each of these patterns of grief—and combinations of them—in their book *Men Don't Cry, Women Do: Transcending Gender Stereotypes of Grief* [19]. In their analysis, they focus not only on the expression of grief, but also on the adaptive strategies that persons experiencing grief choose to deal with their loss [19, pp. 29-53].

There is also an interactive dynamic that often occurs during this phase of processing (though one might also extend it into the phase of *reorganization*). Margaret Stroebe and Henk Schut call it the dual process model of meaning making [20]. At one and the same time, the individual who has experienced a loss oscillates between "loss oriented" and "restoration oriented" experiences in everyday life, moving back and forth, over and over again [21]. In their own words, "The analysis of loss and restoration orientation, the underlying negative and positive cognitions associated with each of these dimensions, and the process of oscillation between these components provide a framework for a systematic probing of assumptive worlds, meaning systems, and life narratives" [20, p. 69].

Although these authors do not explore the use of this model with processing that takes place prior to the occurrence of a loss, there might be validity in utilizing the same interactive oscillation between potential loss orientation and potential resolution orientation. Such an application might also provide further insight into the dynamics of anticipatory grief.

In the phase of processing, both before and after a break in an attachment takes place, it is, however, sometimes quite difficult for an individual to work through feelings (the emotional level) and/or to work out meanings (the intellectual level). It is in one or both of these that an individual can get stuck. As a result, the process of mourning sometimes becomes complicated, even distorted—a topic that is explored in Chapter 5.

EXERCISES FOR READER
AND CAREGIVER

1. Review the exercise that you completed at the end of Chapter 1 in order to be reminded of your attachments. Then, review the exercise you carried out at the end of Chapter 2 in order to remember the breaks in attachments (losses) that you identified.

2. **As a reader** who wants to integrate reading with self-understanding:

    a. Take a sheet of paper and draw an *overview of the process* (see earlier diagram in this chapter), leaving out the words "moving through phases" and the arrows related to those words.

        1) Identify selected breaks in attachments that you are anticipating (in the next year or so), but have not yet occurred, and record them in a word or two in the upper left quadrant.

        2) Then, identify selected breaks in attachments that have occurred recently (in the past year or so) and record them in a word or two in the upper right quadrant.

        3) Reflect on what you have recorded and see if there are insights that emerge.

        4) Share your thoughts and your feelings with another person who is willing to listen and hear what you have to say.

3. **As a caregiver** who wants to understand someone else's life:
   a. Follow the same procedure for that person (on a separate sheet of paper) on the basis of how you perceive that person. Keep in mind that it is important to proceed with caution since this exercise oversimplifies to a considerable extent.
   b. If that relationship is mutual and you want to understand one another's breaks in attachments:
      1) Invite the other person to follow the same procedure (on separate sheets of paper) that you carried out for yourself.
      2) Exchange diagrams and comments in whatever sequence seems most comfortable.
      3) Try to understand each other's breaks in attachments (those that are anticipated and those that have already occurred), both intellectually and emotionally.

4. **As a caregiver** who wants to help others to understand themselves, provide an opportunity for two or more persons to follow the same procedure. Utilize the guidelines given in the exercise at the end of Chapter 1.

5. Find other ways to adapt these exercises in creative and effective ways.

REFERENCES AND NOTES

1. This thesis is an adaptation of the words of Gordon Allport in the preface to V. E. Frankl, *Man's Search for Meaning: An Introduction to Logotherapy* (Rev. Edition), p. 11, Simon and Schuster, New York, 1984, in which he defines the central theme of existentialism, "to live is to suffer, to survive is to find meaning in the suffering."
2. V. E. Frankl, *Ein Psycholog erlebt das Konzentrationslager*, Verlag fur Jugend und Volk, Vienna, 1946.
3. The first English translation was entitled *From Death-Camp to Existentialism: A Psychiatrist's Path to a New Therapy*, Beacon, Boston, 1959. Subsequent editions changed the title to *Man's Search for Meaning* and its translation into other languages.
4. A. D. Prend, *Transcending Loss: Understanding the Lifelong Impact of Grief and How to Make It Meaningful*, Berkley, New York, 1997 (particularly pp. 83-101).
5. C. M. Parkes, *Bereavement: Studies of Grief in Adult Life* (3rd Edition), pp. 7, 43, 66-70, 80, International Universities, Madison, 1998.

6. T. A. Rando, *Treatment of Complicated Mourning,* pp. 30, 33-43, Research, Champaign, 1993.
7. J. Viorst, *Necessary Losses: The Loves, Illusions, Dependencies, and Impossible Expectations That All of Us Have to Give Up in Order to Grow,* Simon and Schuster, New York, 1986.
8. T. Rando, *Clinical Dimensions of Anticipatory Mourning: Theory and Practice in Working with the Dying, the Loved Ones, and Their Caregivers,* Research, Champaign, Illinois, 2000. The term "intimates" is utilized instead of "family," and "concerned others" instead of "friends."
9. E. Lindemann, Symptomatology and Management of Acute Grief, *American Journal of Psychiatry,* 101:2, pp. 141-148, 1944.
10. E. Kübler-Ross, *On Death and Dying,* Macmillan, New York, 1969.
11. E. Kübler-Ross, *Questions and Answers on Death and Dying,* Macmillan, New York, 1974.
12. It was in 1974 that I began to offer my course, "The Meaning of Death," at the University of Indianapolis.
13. T. Attig, *How We Grieve: Relearning the World,* Oxford, New York, 1996.
14. R. A. Neimeyer (ed.), *Meaning Reconstruction and the Experience of Loss,* American Psychological Association, Washington, D.C., 2001.
15. C. B. Wortman and R. Cohen Silver, The Myths of Coping with Loss, *Journal of Consulting and Clinical Psychology,* 56:3, pp. 349-357, 1989. Parkes concurs with the critique of this article [5, p. xiii].
16. R. A. Karaban, *Complicated Losses, Difficult Deaths: A Practical Guide for Ministering to Grievers,* Resource Publications, San Jose, 2000.
17. For additional insights regarding modification of meaning before a break occurs, see K. Doka, Re-creating Meaning in the Face of Illness, in *Clinical Dimensions of Anticipatory Mourning,* pp. 103-113, 2000.
18. R. Neimeyer, *Lessons of Loss: A Guide to Coping,* PsychoEducational Resources, Keystone Heights, Florida, 2000.
19. T. Martin and K. Doka, *Men Don't Cry, Women Do: Transcending Gender Stereotypes,* Brunner/Mazel, New York, 2000.
20. M. Stroebe and H. Schut, Meaning Making in the Dual Process Model of Coping with Bereavement, in *Meaning Reconstruction and the Experience of Loss,* R. A. Neimeyer (ed.), American Psychological Association, Washington, D.C., 2001.
21. See reference 20, diagrams on pp. 59 and 68.

CHAPTER 4

Responding Before the Break
Has Taken Place

Having examined the overall process surrounding breaks in attachments, this chapter will analyze the pattern that emerges *before* a break in a particular attachment takes place. The focus will be upon the individual (the upper left hand quadrant of the diagram utilized in Chapter 3), though references will also be made to others who relate to the individual.

There are patterns that are discernable in the experience of many—though not all—individuals. The most widely known is the one identified by Elisabeth Kübler-Ross as a movement through five stages: denial and isolation, anger, bargaining, depression, and acceptance [1].

Other well-known patterns have been delineated, both prior to and subsequent to Kübler-Ross' analysis. However, they have focused largely on phases that individuals experience *after* a loss has occurred. A representative sampling is considered in the next chapter. Nevertheless, there are some analyses that refer to phases persons go through *before* a loss. They are commonly identified within the framework of "anticipatory grief" [2, p. 180; 3, pp. 83-86; 4, pp. 23-25; 5, p. 78].

Rando provides an historical survey of the last 60 years in the first chapter of her volume *Clinical Dimensions of Anticipatory Mourning: Theory and Practice in Working with the Dying, Their Loved Ones, and Their Caregivers* [6, pp. 1-50]. She also evaluates what she reviews, concludes that there is contradictory research on the subject, and indicates reasons for some of the discrepancies. She then goes on in the second chapter to identify six dimensions of anticipatory grief or, as she calls it, anticipatory mourning: a) *perspective* (patient, intimate, concerned other, caregiver); b) *time focus* (past, present, future); c) *influencing factors* (psychological, social, physiological); d) *major sources of adaptational demands* (loss, trauma); e) *generic operations* (grief and mourning, coping, interaction, psychosocial reorganization, planning, balancing conflicting demands, facilitating an appropriate death); and f) *contextual levels* (intrapsychic, interpersonal, systemic) [6, pp. 51-101].

In this volume, both in preceding and subsequent chapters, the first three dimensions, as well as the sixth, are explicitly included. Parts of the fourth and fifth dimensions are also evident.

A correlation between an individual's experience *before* a break in an attachment occurs and *after* a break is not easily ascertained unless phases are identified in both time frames. The same is true for others (family, friends, caregivers, etc.) as they relate to the individual and to each other. For the place in which an individual ends up in the process before the break is often related to where he or she begins in the process after the break. In other words, the break may occur before an individual moves through all the phases prior to the break, and therefore move him or her to a particular place in the process after the break.

A woman in her mid 30s becomes very angry with her husband for leaving her and filing for a divorce. Months go by. Anguish is intense. Finally the divorce takes place, but the woman does not come to any resolution of the break in her attachment to her husband and thereby has additional grief to work through after the divorce has taken place.

More of this correlation between phases *before* and phases *after* a break will be examined in the synthesis of the process described in Chapter 6.

The phases set forth in this chapter incorporate elements identified by Kübler-Ross; however, there are very substantial differences as well. One such difference is that there is much less emphasis on sequence in this analysis. The phases of anger, bargaining, and depression may be helpful to describe as a logical sequence, yet they often do not flow in such a progression. Also, the last phase is not necessarily one of acceptance. Each of these differences may be due, in part, to the fact that the findings identified by Kübler-Ross come from individuals who are dying, while the findings set forth in this study come from persons dealing with a wider array of loss experiences. They may also be due to the fact that many people do not experience what she is describing.

The pattern that has emerged for this writer from individuals facing breaks in attachments, and from numerous other caregivers who have dealt with persons undergoing such experiences, can be categorized in four phases. The first is an individual's *initial reaction*. It may include shock that is rather mild, quite severe, or somewhere between the two. Factors governing this spectrum of intensity include the degree of attachment, the suddenness of the news, and the consequences of the anticipated break. The mind says, "What?" The gut responds in a manner commensurate with the level of intensity.

In addition there may be confusion present in, or even permeating, this initial reaction. Information may be virtually unavailable, may be incomplete, may be inaccurate, or may not be understood.

Furthermore, there may be a denial of what is being faced. And this denial may be quite firm, particularly if it grows out of a severity of shock. The mind says, "No, it can't be!" The gut responds accordingly. For Kübler-Ross, denial is the first phase, though she incorporates some identification of shock within it. In addition, she attaches isolation to denial, a factor that seems more closely related to individuals who are facing their own death than to those dealing with other types of impending losses.

The second phase before a break in an attachment is *realization*. The individual has reacted initially to whatever has been shared regarding a forthcoming break—whether or not that response has included shock, confusion, and/or denial—and has come to a substantial, though incomplete, realization of what may lie ahead.

The third phase in this analysis is called *processing*. It includes both the emotional and the intellectual; that is, the affective and the cognitive. Each of them comes into focus more and more as realization emerges with increasing clarity. For example, feelings surface viscerally as soon as information pertaining to a break is received; however, they are usually not processed with any significant degree of awareness until an individual begins to realize what may be on the horizon. Likewise, making sense out of such information pertaining to a break is usually not processed until there is sufficient understanding of what is going on.

The sequence within the emotional processing of this phase is not as clear and as fixed as Kübler-Ross indicates, though the phases she identifies as stages two, three, and four are often present. Anger grows out of one's visceral response, as the mind wrestles with the question "Why me?" and the assertion "It's not fair!" Bargaining functions as a respite from the intense feeling of anger as the mind reasons with the prospects of changing what is taking place. "If I get out of this predicament, I promise to . . ." becomes the response, often repeatedly, especially when future circumstances do not seem to change. Depression surfaces in an ever-increasing manner, more focused at first, and then more and more diffused as feelings in one's gut intensify as a result of bargaining not bearing fruit. The mind says, "There's no way out," as it reacts to what has already taken place as well as to what is yet to come.

That such a sequence is sometimes present is certainly the case. However, that it is the pattern that can be anticipated in most individuals does not seem to follow experience. Nevertheless, that the three stages of Kübler-Ross are sometimes present, though in a variety of patterns, is verified by many.

Other emotions in addition to anger and depression are also present in this third phase and therefore need to be processed. Most significant—and often at the core of all other feelings—is fear, particularly fear of what is to come; that is, fear of the future with all of its uncertainties and unknowns. At the center is the fear of losing one's attachments, and more especially, the separation anxiety caused by the fear of losing one's affectional bonds.

At the same time as the individual is working through feelings, he or she is also trying to make some sense of what is happening. The two are intertwined with each other, though some persons are more inclined to grieve in an intuitive manner (emotional processing), while others have a greater tendency to grieve in an instrumental manner (intellectual processing). Those who find themselves grieving more in the latter manner are often engaged in altering their meaning in light of what is taking place. They are not reconstructing their meaning as much as they are modifying it, since the break is somewhat uncertain and still is in the future.

When the third phase has taken place for a significant period of time—if such an amount of time is available—an individual moves to the fourth and final phase before a break in an attachment, namely, *resolution*. It brings the process to some form of conclusion.

However, what the conclusion is often varies from one individual to another. It may be acceptance. Or, it may be defiance; or, resignation; or, some other expression that lies between these ends of the spectrum.

What is being resolved is also a matter for consideration. For some, it is a resolution that is primarily at the emotional level, namely, resolving fear, anger, depression, etc. For others, it is primarily at the intellectual level, namely, resolving the break in a way that provides some meaning to what is happening. While for still others, it is both of these in some combination of the two.

For Kübler-Ross the process is defined in a somewhat rigid manner, rather fixed in a sequential pattern, and, though advocated in a descriptive manner, often received and understood in a prescriptive manner. Her diagram of the process illustrates the stages of dying she developed as she and her colleagues listened to their patients [1, p. 264].

Others have also described phases preceding a break, particularly where there is a life-threatening illness. For example, Karaban, in a chapter entitled "Lingering Losses," identifies five phases of a serious illness: prediagnostic, acute, chronic, temporary recovery, and terminal [4, p. 92; 7]. She is careful, however, to point out that this is not always the case.

Whatever the break may be that is on the horizon, there are broad categories of phases that are common in the overall process, both for the individual and for others who are relating to the individual. In order to visualize them in an overall fashion, a diagram is provided on the next page for the *individual* (the upper left-hand quadrant of the overall diagram in Chapter 3), though the same pattern is also operable for family members, friends, and caregivers who are relating to the individual.

Phases *before* a break in an attachment have been described. That there are variations has already been asserted. However, such variations have not yet been identified. It is to these that this analysis now turns so that the reader will understand that these phases are not rigidly defined, sequentially fixed, or prescriptively set forth.

First, the starting point is not always at the beginning of the process. A break in an attachment may begin so unnoticeably— like the morning dawn—that there is no shock at all. Furthermore, it may develop at such a slow pace—like the cooling of lake temperature in the fall season—that there is very little confusion or denial.

Analysis of the Process:
Before the Break Has Taken Place

INDIVIDUAL

1) initial reaction

→

shock
confusion
denial
etc.

2) realization

— — — — — — →

3) processing

— — — — — — — — — — — →

a) emotional

fear
anger
bargaining
depression
etc.

b) intellectual

meaning modification
etc.

4) resolution

— — — — — — — — — — — — — — — — →

break

in

that

to

which

one

is

attached

A man, age 45, discovers physical symptoms that seem inconsequential at first, but develop with increasing anxiety over a period of months and eventuate in a diagnosis that sets forth a very serious illness.

Second, phases are sometimes repeated. A potential break in an attachment may become clearer and clearer—like a fog that begins to lift—and then the break may become less and less clear and may even be denied—like a fog that settles down and even blocks the view entirely. This is often the case since the break has not yet occurred.

A woman in her early 50s is quite upset when she learns that the company where she works is laying off a large number of employees, is relieved that she is not one of them, is very upset once again a few months later when another round of layoffs is announced, and is relieved once again when she learns that she will stay.

Third, phases may overlap each other. A forthcoming break in an attachment may be realized in part while, at the same time, the response to the break is being emotionally processed in part. That is, there may be both a partial realization and a partial processing taking place at the same time—like the sun that begins to shine before the rain shower is over. Other overlapping may occur between fear and anger, anger and bargaining, or bargaining and depression, etc.

A 13-year-old boy who has been in a very serious accident while riding his bicycle without wearing his helmet lies in his hospital bed with no feeling in both of his legs, realizing, in part, that he may never walk again and expressing, in part, his anger and his rage over what has happened.

Fourth, an individual may be in more than one phase at the same time, though not necessarily because the phases are overlapping. This may occur while the individual is dealing with the same break, namely, denying that the break will occur, as well as expressing fear that the break will occur. It may also take place in a spiral fashion [8, p. 84], while the individual is dealing with different developments of the same break; namely, bringing to resolution one development, as well as realizing that a new one has emerged. Furthermore, it may become evident while the same individual is dealing with different breaks.

A 16-year-old girl denies that the family is going to move to a new community while being really scared that they might have to go. She has stopped dating her boyfriend while realizing that she will also lose other friends if they move. In addition, she is dealing with an intense anger arising from a deep alienation from her parents.

Fifth, an individual may move into the next phase, and then return to the one he or she was in. This may mean that the individual has moved into emotional and/or intellectual processing, but then returns to at least a partial denial, or has moved into resolution and then returns to processing—like the outdoor spring temperature in a northern city that soars to a high in the 70s for a few days only to return to a high in the 30s.

A woman in her late 40s is divorcing her alcoholic husband with whom she has a tentative agreement that has been drafted by each of their respective attorneys regarding a settlement of their affairs, only to learn that he has reneged on several very important items and wants to begin a whole new process of negotiation.

Sixth, an individual needs to move from one phase to another at his or her own pace—like a bird trying to decide if it is safe to come to a group of new feeders that are located very close to a bench on which the family cat sometimes sits. An individual needs to accept the responsibility for how he or she is going to respond to a forthcoming break in an attachment.

A professor who is in his early 70s is failing in health in ways that are increasingly noticeable to others, but denied by him. He is approached by his adult children to consider retiring, while being affirmed in dealing with this matter in his own way.

Seventh, an individual may not move through all the phases. In other words, the break in the attachment may occur while the individual is in any of the phases that may precede the break—like a rain storm that comes when some picnickers in the park have already returned home, when others were planning to leave anyway, when others are in the middle of their meal, and when still others are just arriving.

An employee, age 32, is aware that she is having difficulty performing her responsibilities in a satisfactory manner, but does not believe her job is in jeopardy, when she is called into her supervisor's office and is stunned to learn that she no longer has a job.

Eighth, an individual may come to the break before having reached a substantial degree of resolution. This means that the process is not completed and that the matters that were not resolved prior to the break need to be worked out after the break has taken place—like a group of people on a sailboat cruise that is heading for land, but is several miles from shore when it is struck by a storm packing ferocious winds and rain.

A man who is in his late 60s has become quite ill in a relatively short period of time. He attempts to complete his "unfinished business," but dies before some important matters get resolved.

Ninth, the amount of time spent in a phase will vary. Individuals are different in so many ways (a topic that is discussed in Chapter 6 under the heading of *individual determinants*). So also are the circumstances in which individuals find themselves. Therefore, the process will move more quickly for some and more slowly for others—like cars moving down a highway or students writing an exam.

Two siblings, ages 29 and 32, who are facing the death of their mother respond in very different ways so that they are at quite different places in the process when their mother finally dies.

Tenth, reassessment is repeatedly needed when the timing of the break is unclear. This means that an individual needs to pause and reflect on what is happening in order to understand where one is in the process, and how that understanding may change in direct correlation with how close or how far away the break is, or at least seems to be—like a coach of a number one seeded basketball team that is losing by 14 points in the fourth quarter with less than three minutes to play.

A 12-year-old child is undergoing her fourth surgery to remove a malignant growth from the ventricular system of her brain, with the medical team and the parents unsure of what the outcome will be.

These ten variables do not comprise an exhaustive list. Rather, they are representative of common grief experiences that persons have when they are dealing with a potential break in an attachment—an anticipated loss.

A very important ingredient, however, throughout all the phases of this process is *hope*. It is always available and it can always be experienced, regardless of the circumstances one is in. However, there is a crucial question that must be answered by an individual dealing with a potential break in an attachment, namely, what he or she is hoping for.

One possibility is to hope that the situation is not true. Perhaps wrong information was given. Or, perhaps the wrong interpretation was put on the data that was given or that was heard. And such a hope, if it is not explored, can lead to a denial of what is actually the case.

> *A woman in her late 30s gets a second opinion—and then a third—in order to understand more fully what the medical data says and what it means, so that she can either confirm her hope that the first opinion is wrong, or accept the first opinion as correct and redirect her hope in a new direction.*

A second possibility is to hope that something will occur that will remove the potential break from the horizon. Perhaps something will be discovered that is not presently known. Perhaps a new application of what is already known will be successfully carried out. Or, perhaps an approach will be pursued that is different from all those already in use.

> *A man, age 52, is seriously ill. He hopes for a new medication to be discovered, a new combination of medications to be administered, or a tissue emerging from stem cell research to be implanted, so that his illness can become successfully treated.*

A third possibility is to hope that meaningful experiences will happen during the time that remains before the break occurs. This is a change in the focus of what one is hoping for. It usually comes after one realizes that the situation is true—a break is coming—and that nothing has emerged that will cause the situation to change. However, as one refocuses hope to the meaningful times that can still be experienced, one can also leave the door open for something yet to come that will cause the outlook to change.

A 17-year-old searches for fun times with his friends in the neighborhood, at school, on the tennis team, at church, as well as good times with his family, knowing that he probably has a limited time to live, though also hoping that some medical breakthrough will emerge that will enable him to go on living.

A fourth possibility is to hope that God will receive a person in death and grant him or her everlasting life. Believing in this hope does not negate any of the other three, but it does add a dimension of hope throughout the process as well as when the other three have run their course.

An elderly person has hope for the life to come because she has trusted God very deeply in this life and, therefore, is able to trust God in death and in whatever comes afterward.

The ingredient of hope is regarded as very important to many authors. Kübler-Ross spends a whole chapter on it [1, pp. 138-156]. Donald Capps writes an entire book on it, *Agents of Hope: A Pastoral Psychology,* in which he explores the role of pastors as agents of hope, and claims that "what pastors have uniquely to give others is hope" [9]. Although there is truth in such a statement, it seems to be too lofty a claim. Other caregivers—both professionals and non-professionals—can also function as agents of hope, and can do this with just as much significance as pastors, particularly when they exemplify an authentic faith of their own.

In dealing with this very important theme, Capps identifies and delineates three major threats to hope: despair, apathy, and shame [9, pp. 98-136]. He also points out in some detail three major allies of hope: trust, patience, and modesty [9, pp. 137-162].

Not only does the individual go through phases before a break in an attachment (the upper left-hand quadrant of the diagram), but so do the others who are relating to the individual and/or to whom the individual is relating (the lower left-hand quadrant). All that has been stated in terms of the experience of the individual can also be set forth in regard to the experiences of the others (family, friends, caregivers, etc.). In addition, there are dynamics that take place between the individual and the others, as well as between the others themselves—a topic that is dealt with in Chapter 6.

EXERCISES FOR READER
AND CAREGIVER

1. Review the exercise that you completed at the end of Chapter 2 in order to be reminded of the breaks in attachments (losses) that you identified. Then, review the exercise that you carried out at the end of Chapter 3 in order to remember the overview that you drew and analyzed.

2. **As a reader** who wants to integrate reading with self-understanding:

    a. Take a sheet of paper and draw *an analysis of the process before the break has taken place* (see earlier diagram in this chapter), leaving out the phases that are identified.

    b. Choose a particular break in an attachment that you are anticipating, but that has not yet occurred, and record where you are in the process. Include phases already experienced.

    c. As you do this, reflect on what you have written and see if there are insights that emerge.

    d. Share your thoughts and your feelings with another person who is willing to listen and hear what you have to say.

3. **As a caregiver** who wants to understand someone else's life:

    a. Follow the same procedure for that person (on a separate sheet of paper) on the basis of how you experience that person. Proceed with caution since this exercise oversimplifies to a considerable extent.

    b. If the relationship is mutual and you want to understand the particular breaks that each of you is anticipating:

        1) Invite the other person to follow the same procedure (on separate sheets of paper) that you carried out for yourself.

        2) Exchange diagrams and comments in whatever sequence seems most comfortable.

        3) Try to understand each other's particular break that is anticipated, both intellectually and emotionally.

4. **As a caregiver** who wants to help others to understand themselves, provide an opportunity for two or more persons to follow the same procedure. Utilize the guidelines given in the exercise at the end of Chapter 1.

5. Find other ways to adapt these exercises in creative and effective ways.

REFERENCES AND NOTES

1. E. Kübler-Ross, *On Death and Dying,* Macmillan, New York, 1969.
2. E. Lindemann, Symptomatology and Management of Acute Grief, *American Journal of Psychiatry,* 101:2, 1944.
3. Y. Spiegel, *The Grief Process: Analysis and Counseling,* E. Duke (trans.), Abingdon, Nashville, 1977.
4. R. A. Karaban, *Complicated Losses, Difficult Deaths: A Practical Guide for Ministering to Grievers,* Resource Publications, San Jose, 2000, though she misappropriates Spiegel's four phases.
5. C. M. Parkes, *Bereavement: Studies of Grief in Adult Life* (3rd Edition), International Universities, Madison, 1998, though he is reluctant to embrace this category.
6. T. Rando, *Clinical Dimensions of Anticipatory Mourning: Theory and Practice in Working with the Dying, The Loved Ones, and Their Caregivers,* Research, Champaign, Illinois, 2000.
7. K. Doka, When Illness is Prolonged: Implications for Grief, in *Living with Grief,* K. J. Doka and J. D. Davidson (eds.), pp. 5-15, Taylor & Francis, Bristol, Pennsylvania, 1997.
8. A. D. Prend, *Transcending Loss: Understanding the Lifelong Impact of Grief and How to Make It Meaningful,* Berkley, New York, 1997.
9. D. Capps, *Agents of Hope: A Pastoral Psychology,* Fortress, Minneapolis, 1995.

Analysis of the Process:
After the Break Has Taken Place

break	**OTHERS**
	1) initial reaction
	────────────▶
in	shock numbness denial etc.
that	**2) realization** – – – – – – ────▶
to	**3) processing** – – – – – – – – – ───▶
	a) emotional
which	yearning searching guilt anger depression fear etc.
one	**b) intellectual**
	meaning reconstruction etc.
is	**4) reorganization**
	– – – – – – – – – – – – – ────▶
attached	

after his death, they move on to work through their processing and to reorganize their lives, even though there are periodic episodes that connect with earlier phases.

Second, phases experienced before the break occurred are oftentimes not repeated—like a homeowner who returns from answering the doorbell and continues to plant the bush in the hole that has already been dug. This can be seen in one who has moved beyond realization and has been processing one's emotional and intellectual responses for some time. In such a case, the processing will likely be rather brief after the break, though there may be times when intense feelings still arise or persistent questions resurface.

The adult children of an elderly mother who has had a brain tumor partially removed, followed by months of chemotherapy and radiation treatments, and then a lingering death for nearly three additional years, do not go back to an initial reaction, or to realization, or even to lengthy processing after her death, but go forward by taking steps that will enable them to reorganize their lives without their mother.

Third, a person needs to be encouraged to move through the phases in order to avoid getting bogged down—like a marathon runner who moves to the side of the road to take a cup of water and also receives words of inspiration that motivate him to keep running. This is a bit different than a person progressing strictly at his or her own pace as is the case before a break has taken place. After a break, the person needs to deal with what has happened and move through the phases—not avoid them, or go around them, or even remain alongside them, but go through them.

A man in his mid 40s struggles intensely with the death of his wife and tries to grieve intellectually, month after month after month. He gets bogged down, more and more, until he is encouraged by a friend to express his feelings, to put into words what he is sensing inside, and to release the tears that have been building up inside.

Fourth, an excessive amount of time ought not be spent in any phase—like an individual who is building a cabinet and keeps on measuring the width needed for the top shelf, over and over again. Although the time spent in a particular phase will vary from individual to individual (a topic that is discussed in Chapter 6), there needs to be a movement forward toward the phase of reorganization.

A woman, age 29, is betrayed by her lover and feels her hurt so deeply that she is unable to get over her feelings and, several years later, is still unable to develop a very close relationship with another person, thereby living in relative isolation from others at the very core of her being.

Fifth, a person needs to move through all the phases—like a teenager who thinks about skipping to part four of a final exam after completing the first two parts, but reconsiders and plunges into part three. Persons sometimes think about moving out of realization and going on to reorganization without any processing, emotionally and intellectually, what they have come to understand. It does not work. Grief cannot be carried out apart from sufficient processing.

An employee who is laid off at age 47, due to a buyout of the company for which he works, comes to the realization of what has happened very quickly, even though he is very upset. He tries to reorganize his life without dealing with his feelings about what has happened. As a result, he becomes increasingly irritable and angry in his relationships with his family and with some of his social acquaintances.

Sixth, a person may stop at any point in the process and thereby live with unresolved grief [28]. This may take the form of *postponed* grief—like a student who is failing a course, but chooses not to pick up his or her grades. Or, it may take the form of *prolonged* grief—like a woman with a severe toothache who cancels her appointment with the dentist. Or, it may take the form of *morbid* grief—like a man who covers the glass windows on his home with black paint.

Postponed grief is understood by Rando as a problem of expression [1, pp. 155-167]. It can come about as a result of *absent* grief, in which an individual remains in shock, numbness, and/or denial; however, this is rather rare as an overall and ongoing pattern of behavior. It can also be a result of *delayed* grief, in which an individual slows down the process for any of a variety of reasons over a considerable period of time—even years. In addition, it can also take place as a result of *inhibited* grief, in which an individual restricts the process consciously and/or unconsciously to a significant degree.

A man in his late 30s has incredible difficulty in moving forward in the mourning process, and thereby postpones his grief, as he tries to come to grips with what actually happened three years earlier when the family van he was driving, with his wife and their four young children as passengers, spun on an icy stretch of highway and was struck broadside by a speeding dump truck, killing all members of his family but himself.

Many other examples could be given, some of which would indicate a rather typical postponement of grief, while others would reveal an atypical pattern of behavior.

Prolonged grief is interpreted by Rando as a problem of closure [1, pp. 177-183]. She and others use the term *chronic* to define this pattern of behavior in which mourning persists interminably. The process continues to be replete with intense grief reactions that do not subside and come to their natural conclusion over time. An individual remains in the third phase of emotional and intellectual processing without coming to any substantial degree of release.

A woman's marriage of 21 years comes to an end when her husband dies by suicide. This occurs after he admits a long-term incestuous relationship with their daughter, multiple affairs throughout their marriage, and nothing more than a "make believe love" relationship with his wife over the years. As a result, she is unable to do hardly anything without writhing in pain and anguish, often sobbing uncontrollably, yearning for what she thought she had, despising herself for being fooled, and feeling such despair that the future looks virtually hopeless.

Additional examples could be given that would indicate either a typical or an atypical prolonged grief, or, as is often the case, some combination of the two.

Morbid grief, which is not within the purview of this volume, still needs to be noted as a potential variation. Rando speaks of skewed aspects of mourning and uses the terms *distorted, conflicted,* and/or *unanticipated* to define them [1, pp. 167-177]. In her discussion of distorted mourning, she affirms Lindemann's nine distorted reactions and Raphael's analysis of the patterns of extreme anger and extreme guilt [1, pp. 130-133, 167-171]. In her explication of conflicted mourning, she cites the work of Parkes and

Weiss, particularly their understanding of this type of mourning arising after the loss of a highly troubled, ambivalent relationship [1, pp. 171-174]. In her references to unanticipated mourning, she notes that only Lehrman and, later, Parkes and Weiss, identify this response as a specific syndrome [1, pp. 174-177].

> A mother, whose two childhood daughters died from a rare form of leukemia within the same two-year period nearly a decade ago, lives in a distorted world in which she takes care of two mannequin children in her home. She washes, dresses, and feeds them (makes real food and serves it to them), takes them outside on the porch as weather permits, puts them to bed—day after day after day—talking to them as if her daughters were still living.

Further examples could be given, though such a pursuit would be beyond the scope of this analysis. However, it is important to note that there is an emerging movement that is seeking to define traumatic grief as a disorder. It is explicitly set forth in the book by Selby Jacobs, *Traumatic Grief: Diagnosis, Treatment, and Prevention.* Of particular interest is his utilization of attachment theory as the main framework for thinking about death, grief, and bereavement [29, pp. xv, 1-13].

In each of these categories of postponed, prolonged, or morbid grief, an individual may "get stuck" in the process and thereby live with unresolved grief. Yet, there is one further variation that often is the means by which one can move out of even the most difficult of circumstances.

Seventh, and last, hope may surface, sometimes very slowly at first, and then in an increasing manner, as one moves through the phases—like the sunshine slowly breaking through a gloomy and dismal sky. However, what one hopes for in the phase of reorganization after a break has taken place is somewhat different than what one hopes for in the phase of resolution before a break. No longer does one hope that the situation is not true, or that something will occur that will remove the potential break from the horizon, or that meaningful experiences will happen during the time that remains before the break occurs.

What one hopes for after the break is that meaningful experiences will emerge in an increasing manner as a part of the reorganization process. The break has already happened. The future is open. To be more precise, "hoping," in the words of Capps, is "the perception that what one wants to happen will happen, a perception that is fueled by desire and in response to felt deprivation" [30, pp. 53-64]. "Hopes" are distinguished from hoping in that they are "projections that envision the realizable and thus involve risk" [30, pp. 64-78]. It is the experience of hoping that allows hopes to surface.

It is not an overstatement to say that hope energizes the whole reorganization process. It runs much deeper than optimism. It invigorates those who have experienced a loss.

EXERCISES FOR READER
AND CAREGIVER

1. Review the exercise that you completed at the end of Chapter 2 in order to be reminded of the breaks in attachments (losses) that you identified. Then review the exercise that you carried out at the end of Chapter 3 in order to remember the overview that you drew and analyzed.

2. **As a reader** who wants to integrate reading with self-understanding:

    a. Take a sheet of paper and draw *an analysis of the process after the break has taken place* (see earlier diagram in this chapter), leaving out the phases that are identified. This will be similar to the exercise you completed at the end of Chapter 4.

    b. Choose a particular break in an attachment that you have already experienced, and record where you are in the process. Include phases already experienced.

    c. As you do this, reflect on what you have written and see if there are insights that emerge.

    d. Share your thoughts and your feelings with another person who is willing to listen and hear what you have to say.

3. **As a caregiver** who wants to understand someone else's life:

    a. Follow the same procedure (on a separate sheet of paper) on the basis of how you experience that person. Proceed with caution since this exercise oversimplifies to a considerable extent.

    b. If the relationship is mutual and you want to understand the particular breaks that each of you is experiencing:

1) Invite the other person to follow the same procedure (on separate sheets of paper) that you carried out for yourself.
2) Exchange diagrams and comments in whatever sequence seems most comfortable.
3) Try to understand each other's particular break that has already occurred, both intellectually and emotionally.

4. **As a caregiver** who wants to help others to understand themselves, provide an opportunity for two or more persons to follow the same procedure. Utilize the guidelines given in the exercise at the end of Chapter one.

5. Find other ways to adapt these exercises in creative and effective ways.

REFERENCES AND NOTES

1. T. Rando, *Treatment of Complicated Mourning,* Research, Champaign, 1993, wherein she examines the theories of leading researchers in her historical overview (from Freud to Zisook), pp. 79-149.
2. M. Stroebe, R. Hansson, W. Stroebe, and H. Schut (eds.), *Handbook of Bereavement Research: Consequences, Coping, and Care,* American Psychological Association, Washington, D.C., 2001.
3. C. M. Parkes, *Bereavement: Studies of Grief in Adult Life* (3rd Edition), International Universities, Madison, 1998.
4. J. Bowlby, *Loss: Sadness and Depression,* Basic Books, London, 1980. The first phase was not initially included as a separate one.
5. P. Marris, The Social Construction of Uncertainty, in *Attachment Across the Life Cycle,* pp. 77-90, Routledge, London, 1991.
6. P. Marris, *Loss and Change,* Routledge, London, 1986.
7. P. Marris, *Meaning and Action,* Routledge, London, 1987.
8. A. Wolfelt, *Understanding Your Grief: Ten Essential Touchstones for Finding Hope and Healing Your Heart,* Companion, Fort Collins, Colorado, 2003.
9. N. Reeves, *A Path Through Loss: A Guide to Writing Your Healing and Growth,* Northstone, Kelona, British Columbia, 2001.
10. J. Guntzelman, *God Knows You're Grieving: Things to Do to Help You Through,* Sorin, Notre Dame, Indiana, 2001.
11. R. Moody and D. Arcangel, *Life After Loss: Conquering Grief and Finding Hope,* HarperCollins, San Francisco, 2001.
12. V. Parachin, *Healing Grief,* Chalice, St. Louis, 2001.
13. B. Deits, *Life After Loss: A Personal Guide Dealing with Death, Divorce, Job Change and Relocation* (3rd Edition), Fisher, Tucson, 2000.

14. M. Dunn, *The Good Grief Guide: How to Come through Bereavement with Hope for the Future and at Peace with the Past,* Pathways, Oxford, 2000.
15. D. Smith and T. Chapin, *Spiritual Healing: A Handbook of Activities, Guided Imagery, Meditations, and Prayers,* Psycho-Spiritual Publications, Madison, Wisconsin, 2000.
16. W. E. Oates, *Grief, Transition, and Loss: A Pastor's Practical Guide,* Fortress, Minneapolis, 1997.
17. A. Davis Prend, *Transcending Loss: Understanding the Lifelong Impact of Grief and How to Make It Meaningful,* Berkley, New York, 1997.
18. M. Lawrenz and D. Green, *Life After Grief: How to Survive Loss and Trauma,* Baker, Grand Rapids, 1995.
19. N. Leich and M. Davidsen-Nielsen, *Healing Pain: Attachment, Loss and Grief Therapy,* D. Stoner (trans.), Routledge, London, 1991.
20. T. Rando, *How to Go on Living When Someone You Love Dies,* Bantam, New York, 1991.
21. G. Westberg, *Good Grief: A Constructive Approach to the Problem of Loss,* Fortress, Philadelphia, 1962.
22. J. W. Worden, *Grief Counseling and Grief Therapy: A Handbook for the Mental Health Practitioner* (3rd Edition), Springer, New York, 2002.
23. R. A. Neimeyer, *Meaning Reconstruction and the Experience of Loss,* American Psychological Association, Washington, D.C., 2001.
24. D. Klass, P. R. Silverman, and S. L. Nickman (eds.), *Continuing Bonds: New Understandings of Grief,* Taylor & Francis, Philadelphia, 1996.
25. D. Klass, *The Spiritual Lives of Bereaved Parents,* Brunner/Mazel, Philadelphia, 1999.
26. D. Klass, The Inner Representation of the Dead Child in the Psychic and Social Narratives of Bereaved Parents, in *Meaning Reconstruction and the Experience of Loss,* pp. 77-94, American Psychological Association, Washington, D.C., 2001.
27. G. Hagman, Beyond Decathexis: Toward a New Psychoanalytic Understanding and Treatment of Mourning, in *Meaning Reconstruction and the Experience of Loss,* pp. 13-31, American Psychological Association, Washington, D.C., 2001.
28. P. Boss, *Ambiguous Loss: Learning to Live with Unresolved Grief,* Harvard, Cambridge, 1999.
29. S. Jacobs, *Traumatic Grief: Diagnosis, Treatment, and Prevention,* Brunner/Mazel, Philadelphia, 1999.
30. D. Capps, *Agents of Hope: A Pastoral Psychology,* Fortress, Minneapolis, 1995.

CHAPTER 6

Responding in a Personal Way

The patterns that are common to many persons in their process of mourning have been considered in the three preceding chapters, first as an overview (Chapter 3) and then in greater detail (before the break in Chapter 4 and after the break in Chapter 5). In this chapter the focus is on those determinants that make every person's experience of grief unique.

In order to understand those individual determinants as fully as possible within the overall framework that has already been examined, a synthesis that incorporates all four quadrants is provided. In structural form, it is similar to the overview given in Chapter 3, but it incorporates the analyses set forth in Chapters 4 and 5. In doing so, the dissimilarities between the left and right sides, as well as the top and bottom sections, become more evident.

In regard to the left and right sides, there is *confusion* rather than *numbness* associated with *shock* before the break since the shock is not as intense before the break as it sometimes is after the break. Second, the *processing* before the break differs from the *processing* after the break in that there is no *bargaining* after the break since the break has already occurred. Third, there is no *yearning* or *searching* before the break since the attachment is not yet broken. Fourth, there is less guilt, or no guilt at all, before the break since it has not yet taken place. Fifth, there is modification of the meaning before the break, but reconstruction of the meaning after the break. Sixth, the *reorganization* after the break differs from the *resolution* before the break since the individual moves on to cultivate other attachments and/or establish new attachments, as well as maintain some continuity with the attachment that has broken.

In regard to the top and bottom sections, the *individual* and the *others* often go through the same phases, except when the break is a death. In that case, what the individual actually experiences is unknown, though what others experience is known. In breaks other than a death, such as a divorce or the loss of a job, both the individual and the others go through similar phases. Second, the others need to be aware of where they are in the process as they also seek to understand where the individual is. Third, the others are often, though not always, behind the individual when the break has not yet occurred. Fourth, the others are often, though not always, ahead of the individual when the break has already occurred.

The diagram that follows on the next page seeks to illustrate this overall synthesis. It incorporates all four quadrants while only a single quadrant was utilized in the diagram in Chapters 4 and 5. Furthermore, it invites the reader to supply the terms from the diagrams previously delineated, repeating in the lower left-hand quadrant what was earlier used in the upper left-hand quadrant, as well as repeating in the upper right-hand quadrant what was earlier used in the lower right-hand quadrant (except in the case of a death).

Utilizing the four quadrants of the diagram to analyze one's own experience and/or the experience of others provides opportunities for insights to emerge that might otherwise be more difficult to discern.

A professor is sitting at a dinner table with a few colleagues from the university, when one of them says she is so surprised that Charles, who is in his mid 50s, is already going out with a woman, just three months after his wife died. The professor asks if they knew Susan, Charles' wife, and how she died. They respond by saying that she died from some type of terminal illness, though they don't know the details. The professor explains that Susan died of cancer, after undergoing major surgery and almost two years of chemotherapy. The professor then takes a felt pen and draws a diagram (the one utilized as an overview in Chapter 3 of this volume, and now utilized as a synthesis in this chapter) on his paper napkin. He goes on to point out the following: 1) that Susan had been in the upper left-hand quadrant, working through her grief as she was facing an impending death; 2) that Charles had been in the lower left-hand quadrant, working through his grief as

Synthesis of the Process

INDIVIDUAL	break	
1)		1)
2)	in	2)
3)		3)
a)	that	a)
b)		b)
4)	to	4)
OTHERS	which	
1)		1)
2)	one	2)
3)		3)
a)		a)
b)	is	b)
4)	attached	4)

he was responding to Susan's expected death; 3) that the professor himself had been in the lower left-hand quadrant, working through his grief as he interacted with Susan and Charles; 4) that colleagues in the university community— particularly those who knew her fairly well, but didn't have close contact with Susan during her illness—had also been in the lower left-hand quadrant, though may not have moved very far along in processing their feelings; 5) that Susan was now dead; 6) that Charles had almost completed the grieving process before Susan died; 7) that the professor had moved along with Susan and Charles, though sometimes ahead and sometimes behind each of them; and 8) that the colleagues from the university seated around the table needed to identify where they were in the lower right-hand quadrant.

Discussion follows and, without the professor having to explain anything further, one colleague says, "I guess Charles is ready to move on since he has already grieved for over two years. We're not ready to let him, since we haven't moved as far in our grieving over the loss of Susan as Charles has done. And we're using where we are in the process to make judgments about Charles and what he is doing." Silence falls over the group. The professor knows it is time to listen. Then a second colleague says, "Very interesting. And we thought we were so right in our interpretation." Silence comes again. Then, after a pause, the professor quietly speaks and says, "Charles seems to be in the process of reorganizing his life. Perhaps we need to understand that. Perhaps we also need to interact with Charles and let him tell us where he's been, where he is, and where he's heading." Heads nod. Eyes make contact. Gentle smiles are exchanged.

Although phases that many persons experience can be identified, and variations regarding those phases can be described, there is no analysis that can take into account all of the experiences that are unique to a particular individual dealing with a particular loss. Wayne Oates delineates this point very precisely in his book *Your Particular Grief* [1]. He makes it clear that the loss a person experiences is *his or her loss* and the grief that person experiences is *his or her particular grief* [1, p. 15]. The "shapers" of grief that he identifies are: 1) the person's unique relationship to the loss; 2) the manner of the loss; 3) the person's previous experience with grief; 4) the timeliness or untimeliness of the loss; and 5) the spiritual resources of the mourner [1, pp. 16-21].

Determinants of grief are described in some detail by Parkes in *Bereavement: Studies of Grief in Adult Life*. In his first edition (1972), he devotes one chapter to them. However, in his third edition (1998) his presentation has been expanded to three chapters: 1) relationship, gender, and age [2, pp. 117-128]; 2) mode of death [2, pp. 129-138]; and 3) personal vulnerability [2, pp. 139-160]. These categories are the focal points he examines, though he lists a number of others in an outline entitled "determinants of the outcome of bereavement." The structure of that outline is based on time differentiation as denoted by the words antecedent, concurrent, and subsequent [2, p. 118].

Worden also delineates determinants of grief. He refers to them as "mediators of mourning" [3, pp. 37-45]. Although they are not organized in the categories that Parkes utilizes, he nevertheless does speak of "historical antecedents" and "concurrent stresses" among the seven categories that structure his analysis.

Rando speaks of "determinants and associated factors" in her analysis of symptoms and syndromes in complicated outcomes of loss [4, pp. 149-183]. Furthermore, she also utilizes the categories of prior, concurrent, and subsequent in her examination of variables that may influence an individual's response, especially in the identification of factors predictive of complicated mourning [4, pp. 158, 160-161, 163-165, 168-169, 172-173, 176, 178-181].

The utilization of these overall categories to delineate the determinants of a particular person's response will structure the analysis that follows. First, those determinants that occur *prior to the break* will be examined. Then, those that are present *at the time of the break* (as well as prior to and after the break) will be analyzed. Finally, those determinants that take place *after the break* will be considered.

The individual determinants that occur **prior to the break** can be identified in four categories. The first and most important one is the *development of attachments* that have taken place from infancy to the time of the break. They include relationships that have been given (e.g., parents and siblings), that have been sought (e.g., friends), and that have occurred by circumstance (e.g., neighbors, schoolmates, fellow-employees). More important, they include those relationships that have developed into attachments. And most important, they include those attachments that have developed into affectional bonds (see Chapter 1).

> *A woman in her mid 40s has a very loving mother who was her primary caregiver during infancy and childhood, and thereby her deepest affectional bond. Quite unexpectedly she learns that her mother is terminally ill and reacts to her in a very different manner than to her neighbor across the street who also is terminally ill.*

A second determinant comprises the experiences a person has had with *previous breaks.* This does not only encompass the number of breaks and the types of breaks—important as both of these are—but also the way the person has dealt with previous breaks.

> *A man who is laid off due to his company being purchased by a competitor responds quite differently if this is the first or the third time he has been forced to leave employment, as well as if this loss is on top of an earlier divorce that he didn't want. Yet, even more important, how this man responded to these former losses significantly impacts how he responds to the current lay off.*

A third one is the *degree of attachment* that a person has toward other individuals, things, places, events, and a variety of intangibles (see Chapter 2). The stronger the attachment, the more grief is experienced as a result of a break in that attachment.

> *A college senior who becomes aware that her male friend and lover for the past three years has betrayed her trust and has had sex with her sorority sister is quite different from the sorority sister involved in this episode who thinks it is a one-time thing that no one else will ever know about.*

A fourth determinant that is influential prior to the break is the *manner in which the break in the attachment occurs.* It may be sudden and unexpected, or it may be gradual and anticipated over a long period of time.

> *Parents who receive a phone call indicating their teenage son has been killed in a car wreck react differently from another set of parents who learn that their teenage son has a life-threatening illness.*

In addition to the individual determinants that develop and take place **prior to the break** in an attachment, there are a number that are influential **at the time of the break**. One is the *age* of the individual. Whether one is an infant, a child, a teenager, a young adult, a mid-career adult, or an older adult influences how one understands and responds to a break.

A young child who is abandoned by his mother responds in a very different way than a mid-career woman who is abandoned by her highly successful husband.

A second one is the *gender* of the individual [5, pp. 99-112]. Whether one is a woman or a man often—though not always—impacts how one deals with a loss. The extent to which this is true is a combination of one's genes, one's cultural conditioning, and the interactions between them. Nevertheless, a number of studies have shown that women and men frequently demonstrate patterns of responses that are dissimilar from one another [5, pp. 169-177, 179-181].

A mother in her early 30s grieves both emotionally and intellectually, expressing her feelings as well as her thoughts, about the death of her young daughter due to leukemia, while her husband tries to grieve intellectually and buries his feelings. As a result, he lives with unresolved grief that affects—knowingly and unknowingly—his relationships with others, even his wife.

A third determinant is the *type of personality* that the individual exemplifies [5, pp. 87-97]. If a person is an outgoing type that receives energy from interacting with others (an E or extrovert on the Myers-Briggs Type Inventory), that individual is more likely to seek out others, share with them, and be energized by the interaction. Whereas, if one is a more reserved type that is energized by spending time apart from others (an I on the Inventory), that individual is more likely to find time alone to regain energy and strength. Each type on this scale—as well as the other scales and the varied combinations that are possible even within each of the scales—will therefore respond to a break in an attachment according to the profile that is uniquely its own.

A man in his early 40s leaves his old neighborhood that he loves very much and moves to a new community. Indicative of his being a type E personality, he repeatedly takes the initiative to seek out his new neighbors and become acquainted. As a result of being a type I, his wife spends considerable time at home, though she does reach out to neighbors on occasion.

A fourth one is the *attitudinal* stance that an individual takes toward a break in an attachment. If a person is basically optimistic and positive toward life, he or she will look for the good things and see them as indicators of encouragement. While, on the other hand, if a person is basically pessimistic and negative toward life, he or she will lean in the direction of the bad things and see them as signs of discouragement.

A high school student receives a very low passing grade on an essay exam and assumes the grade will be better on the next exam, while another student receives the same grade and assumes the grade on the next exam may not even be passing.

A fifth determinant is the *physical condition* of the individual. Whether one is in excellent health, in reasonable health, or in poor health influences how one will deal with a break in an attachment.

A widower who is facing retirement in a few months and is in excellent health looks forward to its opportunities quite differently than the widower who is coming up to his retirement at the same time, but is in poor health and is dreading the idea of being home alone.

A sixth one is the *emotional stability and mental health* of an individual. The degree to which a person is stable and healthy psychologically will impact the way he or she responds to an experience of loss.

While a family is away on a winter vacation, an upstairs water pipe bursts and floods the two main levels of the house as well as the finished basement, causing tens of thousands of dollars in damage. One parent is a very stable person, while the other is not, leading to very different responses to the devastating loss.

A seventh determinant is the *sexual orientation* of the individual. A heterosexual man or woman can deal openly in virtually any setting with a break in a serious relationship, while a gay man or a lesbian woman has a very limited context in which to deal with such a break since the relationship is often unknown, unrecognized, or disapproved.

A lesbian woman who has been betrayed by her lover as a result of her lover breaking off a six-year deep and intimate relationship finds it difficult to grieve in a number of public contexts since many persons do not know about their relationship, or do not recognize it, or do not approve of it.

An eighth one is the *educational level* of the individual. Whether a person dropped out of school at an early age, completed high school, received a college degree, went on for a master's degree, or earned a doctorate, will often—though not always—affect the way in which a person understands and responds to a loss.

A young man in his mid 20s who dropped out of school at age 14, with limited awareness of what grief is and how persons can respond, reacts in a very different manner than another young man of a similar age who earned both a bachelor's and a master's degree in behavioral science from an outstanding educational institution.

A ninth determinant that is influential at the time of the break, as well as prior to and after the break, is the *race* of the individual. If one is European American (i.e., Caucasian), one has numerous privileges that often are assumed by such persons in the United States. This is not the case for other races, particularly African Americans who have to deal with rampant racism in so many of their interactions in society.

A company downsizes and lays off a large number of hourly employees. Some are European American, some are Latin American, and some are African American. As they go out to look for new jobs, the issue of race influences the process far more often for the African Americans, and even the Latin Americans, than for the European Americans.

A tenth one is the *cultural context* of the individual [5, pp. 113-121; 6]. Expressions of grief will vary from one culture to another as well as within each culture itself. Native American, Asian American, Latin American, African American, and European American communities each have their own expressions that grow out of their own heritage, with multiple variations within each of these communities.

An elderly woman who is a Korean immigrant dies at home early one morning. Her body remains there and her family and close friends come to visit. At the funeral the next day, her two daughters wear white clothes and no make-up. Her son and son-in-law wear black suits with white armbands.

An eleventh determinant is the *belief and value system* of the individual. If a person believes there is a God, and that God can be trusted in this life as well as in the life to come, that person can view death as a transition from one life to the next in contrast to a person who has no such belief and views death as the end of the road.

An elderly man who is terminally ill is at peace with himself and with those near to him as a result of experiencing a deep peace in his relationship with God who will soon receive him in death.

A twelfth one is the *occupation* of the individual. The extent to which a person has a caring group of colleagues at work who understand the dynamics of a break in a significant attachment is the extent to which he or she can be assisted in dealing with it.

A mother whose 15-year-old son is randomly murdered on a street corner returns to her job in a social service agency and receives incredible care, while the father returns to his office in a brokerage firm and, after brief greetings, is urged by his supervisor to process the backlog of paperwork.

A thirteenth determinant is the *social circumstance* of the individual. Whether one is a part of the lower class, the lower middle class, the middle class, the upper middle class, or the upper class (however one understands these terms) will influence how one responds to a break in an attachment.

A mid career man who loses his job when his company decides to relocate doesn't know what to do since his opportunities are very limited by his lower middle class circumstance, while the head of his plant pursues several promising opportunities to find a new position.

A fourteenth one is the *geographical location* of the individual. If a person lives in a small town where almost everyone knows everyone else, or in a suburban community where peer pressure abounds, or in an urban setting where impersonalization often runs rampant, that location will impact the way in which a person deals with a loss.

> *A house in a small town catches fire one evening when the family is away and burns to the ground. When the family returns they are greeted by other family members, as well as many neighbors and friends, who share in their anguish, hug them, cry with them, show compassion to them, offer them places to stay, food to eat, and much more.*

A fifteenth determinant is the *financial security* of the individual. Whether one has very limited resources, ample resources, or abundant resources makes a difference in what one can draw upon to respond to a break in an attachment.

> *A man, age 39, walks out on his wife and their three young children because he has developed a relationship with another woman. His wife, age 38, takes immediate action by changing the locks on all the doors, transferring substantial resources from old to new bank accounts, removing valuables from safe deposit boxes, calling her accountant, hiring an attorney, etc., etc., etc.—all before her husband finds out about her first move—since she has the awareness of what to do and the financial resources to carry out these actions.*

A sixteenth one is the *support system* that the individual has. If there are only a few people to respond to a person who has experienced a serious loss, or a larger yet limited number, or a very substantial number, it makes a difference in terms of the support the individual will receive.

> *A single parent in her mid 50s is stunned to learn that her son has been killed in a plane crash while out of the country. As word spreads, her family responds, together with a number of church members, friends, neighbors, and co-workers.*

A seventeenth determinant is the *full range of attachments* that an individual has. This includes all that really matters:

relationships with others, things, places, events, and a variety of intangibles (see Chapter 2).

A woman who is her own person as well as a wife, a mother, and a grandmother, reflects on what really matters in each of these categories and thereby becomes aware of the resources that she has when responding to a loss.

An eighteenth one that is influential at the time of the break, as well as prior to and after the break, is *the extent to which the individual utilizes his or her freedom to respond.*

A man who knows he has some degree of freedom to respond to the circumstances he is in, and who acts on that knowledge, is quite different than either the man who doesn't know he has that freedom, or the man who knows, but doesn't act on what he knows.

In addition to those individual determinants that develop and take place **prior to the break** in an attachment, and those that are influential **at the time of the break**, there are also those that occur **after the break**. They can be identified in five categories. The first one is *available alternatives*. Whether one has been empowered with numerous options from which to choose, or only a very limited number of options, makes a considerable difference in how one deals with a break in an attachment. Although one always has some degree of freedom to choose how he or she will respond, it is far less difficult if there are a variety of possibilities.

A very gifted woman is laid off from her job, but is not deeply dejected, since she chose her position from three that were offered to her at three different companies at the time she was hired. She believes she will find a new position in a short amount of time. At the same time, another woman is laid off at the same company and becomes very frightened and troubled because she is not a highly skilled person and had such a hard time finding the job she has just lost.

A second determinant is *other breaks* that have recently taken place, or are taking place at the same time, or are likely to take place in the near future. At times all three of these types are present, while at other times one or two take place. Regardless, the individual is impacted by other breaks that are in close proximity in time.

A professor is retiring. He meets his class and bids farewell to his last group of students. The next day he goes to his office and struggles a great deal as he clears out his files, throwing out many student records and related materials. He brings home many personal belongings in the days that follow and puts them together with other items he is packing in preparation for his move to a new location where many of his friends and family will not be living. He pauses to realize the several losses he is experiencing at the same time.

A third one is *responses* a person receives from others as he or she deals with a break that has taken place. This depends, first of all, on the number of responses received. Yet, it also depends on the quality of those responses. Furthermore, there are a vast variety of interactions, ranging from those that are quite helpful to those that are downright destructive.

A woman in her late 40s goes through a long, drawn out, messy divorce. Since she is well known in the community, in her church, and in her neighborhood, a number of people respond to her, especially when the divorce is finalized. Some, particularly those in her neighborhood, are very supportive and helpful while others, particularly those in her church, are quite judgmental and condemning.

A fourth determinant is *barriers* that may confront a person who is responding to a break. Although there are many types of barriers, there is one category that is particularly significant. Kenneth Doka identifies losses that cannot be acknowledged openly, mourned publicly, or supported socially, and calls them experiences of "disenfranchised grief" [7, pp. 3-11]. In his earlier analysis (1989), he cites three situations in which they often occur, namely, *unrecognized relationships* (e.g., biological parents of adopted children, homosexual relationships, ex-spouses, past lovers, former friends, or roommates in nursing homes), *unacknowledged losses* (e.g., abortions, perinatal deaths, adoptions, placement of children in foster care, losing a pet, or experiencing a psychosocial death as when a partner develops some form of mental illness), and *excluded grievers* (e.g., children who are thought to be too young to grieve, adults who are considered too old, or persons with a developmental disability who are excluded in a variety of ways) [7, pp. 5-7].

A man lives with a partner who has AIDS. Over time the illness causes deterioration, slowly yet steadily, until death occurs. Mourning that was difficult while his partner was living is now even more difficult since what was not acknowledged openly or validated socially cannot now be easily carried out publicly.

In his more recent analysis (2002), Doka adds two additional categories, namely, the circumstances of the death, and the way individuals grieve [8, pp. 5-22; 9, pp. 39-60].

A fifth determinant that is influential after the break involves the *complications* that may arise in one's response to a break in an attachment. Some of these have been identified as postponed, prolonged, or morbid grief. Karaban deals with them as a pastoral counselor. Rando analyzes them in greater detail as a clinical psychologist. Yet both set forth ways of ministering to grievers and/or treating individuals with serious complications as well as those complications that are much more commonplace.

A teenager who is a senior in high school has lost her best friend through a tragic motorcycle accident. She expresses her pain and anguish, over and over again. A classmate says—and keeps on saying—"Don't feel like that." As a result, the teenager stops expressing what she feels, gets out of touch with her true feelings, and then feels increasingly guilty for what she has been saying. Her grief is beginning to develop serious complications.

Individual determinants in responding to a break in an attachment are many in number. They combine to form a process of mourning that is unique to each human being as he or she moves through a series of phases. As that process unfolds, the determinants need to be grasped and internalized by the griever as his or her own. They must also be respected, understood, and accepted by the caregiver as he or she responds to an individual and/or a group dealing with a break in an attachment.

In order to assist a person in processing his or her individual grief, there are a number of personal applications that may be utilized. Neimeyer delineates a number of them that are particularly appropriate following a break in an attachment. Included in his summation are the following: biographies, drawings/paintings, epitaphs, journals, life imprints, linking objects, loss characterizations, meaning reconstruction interviews, memory books, metaphoric images, metaphoric stories, personal pilgrimages, photo galleries, poetry of loss, reflective reading, ritualization, and unsent letters [10, pp. 127-207].

The caregiver who is aware of these and other options, and who discerns the ways in which a particular person is attempting to process his or her grief, can then correlate one or more of these applications with the manner in which the person is dealing with his or her break in attachment. In addition, there are the exercises at the end of each chapter in this volume that are designed to integrate reading with understanding, both of oneself and others for whom one provides care.

EXERCISES FOR READER
AND CAREGIVER

1. Prior to completing the exercises that follow, make a copy of the diagram in this chapter (or draw a copy if that is more convenient). Then, from memory, as much as possible, write the words set forth in this volume that coincide with the numbers and letters, completing all four quadrants of the diagram. Compare your responses with the terms used in the diagrams in Chapters 3 and 4. Reflect on what you recorded—both from memory and from further checking—to see learning that has taken place.

2. Review the drawing that you completed at the end of Chapter 3 in order to be reminded of the overview that you analyzed. Then review the exercises that you carried out at the end of Chapters 4 and 5 in order to remember the particular breaks that you identified.

3. **As a reader** who wants to integrate reading with self-understanding:

    a. Take a sheet of paper and draw a synthesis of the process (see earlier diagram in this chapter), leaving out the numbers, letters, arrows, and dashes. It should look the same as the diagram that you drew in exercise #2 at the end of the third chapter (and may even become the framework that you will regularly use to process loss experiences in your own life as well as those in the lives of others).

     b. Identify a break that involves both an individual and others relating to the individual (including yourself in either or neither of these categories), as well as a break that begins with anticipatory grief, but continues after the break takes place. In other words, choose a break that involves all four quadrants of the diagram.

     c. Utilizing your own analytical skills, record words, dashes, arrows, etc. so that the process of grief can be depicted with as much insight as possible.

     d. In order to test your understanding with another trusted colleague:

       1) Share what you have recorded and what your interpretation is.

       2) Ask that person to respond to the conclusions to which you have come.

       3) Listen carefully and be prepared to revise what you have recorded if you hear other ways of describing the situation that make sense to you.

4. **As a caregiver** who wants to understand someone else's life:

     a. Follow the same procedure for that person (on a separate sheet of paper) on the basis of how you experience that person. Proceed with caution.

     b. If the relationship is mutual and you want to understand each others responses:

       1) Invite another colleague (on a separate sheet of paper) to diagram and interpret the response of grief and mourning resulting from an experience of loss.

       2) Respond to the conclusion to which that person has come by asking questions and by giving reflective feedback.

       3) Try to hear what is being said before sharing alternative ways of viewing the experiences being described.

5. **As a caregiver** who wants to help others understand their own experiences of grief, provide an opportunity for a group of persons to follow the same procedure and/or respond to what one individual shares (whether you are the person who shares, or the one who provides the opportunity for another person to share).

6. Find other ways to adapt these exercises in creative and effective ways.

REFERENCES AND NOTES

1. W. Oates, *Your Particular Grief,* Westminster, Philadelphia, 1981.
2. C. M. Parkes, *Bereavement of Grief in Adult Life* (3rd Edition), International Universities, Madison, 1998.
3. J. W. Worden, *Grief Counseling and Grief Therapy: A Handbook for the Mental Health Practitioner* (3rd Edition), Springer, New York, 2002.
4. T. Rando, *Treatment of Complicated Mourning,* Research, Champaign, 1993.
5. T. Martin and K. Doka, *Men Don't Cry, Women Do: Transcending Gender Stereotypes,* Brunner/Mazel, New York, 2000.
6. K. Nader, N. Dubrow, and B. Hudnall Stamm (eds.), *Honoring Differences: Cultural Issues in the Treatment of Trauma and Loss,* Brunner/Mazel, Philadelphia, 1999.
7. K. Doka, Disenfranchised Grief, in *Disenfranchised Grief: Recognizing Hidden Sorrow,* K. Doka (ed.), Lexington Books, Lexington, 1989.
8. K. Doka, Introduction, in *Disenfrancised Grief: New Directions, Challenges, and Strategies for Practice,* K. Doka (ed.), Research Press, Champaign, 2002.
9. C. Corr, Revisiting the Concept of Disenfranchised Grief, in *Disenfranchised Grief: New Directions, Challenges, and Strategies for Practice,* K. Doka (ed.), Research Press, Champaign, 2002.
10. R. Neimeyer, *Lessons of Loss: A Guide to Coping,* PsychoEducational Resources, Keystone Heights, Florida, 2000.

CHAPTER 7

Being Transformed Through Responses

The thesis of this book, formulated initially in Chapter 3, states that survival is dependent upon a person learning how to respond to the breaks in attachments that he or she experiences in life. It is expanded in Chapters 4 and 5 in terms of what is commonly experienced before and after a break takes place. It is then developed in Chapter 6 from the perspective of an individual responding in his or her own particular way.

In this chapter the thesis is taken one step further. It asserts that all human beings will change as they respond to breaks in attachments. No one is left out and no other option is given. Responding necessitates and enables change!

Whether that transformation is positive or negative, it is nevertheless a transformation. It may be a pattern of responses that is basically positive, basically negative, or a complex mixture of the two. Or, more likely, it may be a pattern that develops over a period of time, with fluctuations in accordance with one's maturation process. In that case, it will not form quickly or easily. It will, rather, develop as one moves—hopefully—toward a more and more wholesome and meaningful way of life. And, because it takes a lot of time and energy to develop, it will also not go away quickly or easily. Likewise, if one moves in a direction that is away from such a way of life, it will also take a lot of time and energy to work out a substantial redirection of life.

Transformation takes time. It doesn't often happen through one event. It usually takes place as a result of one event added to a second event, added to a third event, added to countless other events, until a pattern emerges. And in each of those events, decisions are made in response to the situation in which a person finds himself or herself.

In terms of responses to a break in an attachment, Attig, in his book *How We Grieve: Relearning the World,* develops the thesis that grieving is active, not passive [1, pp. 25-62]. This means that an individual needs to accept responsibility for how he or she is going to respond, and then make choices across the spectrum from the most minimal to the most strategic. In doing so, the individual who is dealing with a loss enters into a process of relearning the world. This process does not focus on learning new information about the world, but learning how to be and how to act in the world differently, as a result of a loss [1, p. 107]. The spheres in which this occurs include one's physical surroundings, one's relationships with others, and, most importantly, one's self.

This understanding of grieving as something active is, in principle, the same point as that made by Frankl (see beginning of Chapter 3). The individual has some degree of freedom to respond—regardless of what the break is—and by exercising that freedom has the opportunity to accept the responsibility to act in a way that will lead to a wholesome and meaningful life. Whether he or she accepts this responsibility is up to the individual.

Transformation is the inevitable result of such a decision, whatever it is. The individual does not remain the same. Likewise, the world in which the individual lives does not stay the same. In short, life is not the same.

> *A young boy breaks his leg as a result of falling from a branch of one of the trees in his backyard. He and his world are not the same.*

Transformation in this instance is likely temporary. However, in some situations transformation is permanent. Not only is the individual and the world in which he or she lives different, it will never return to the way it was.

> *A young girl is struck by a car as she is crossing the street in front of her home. She nearly dies, but as a result of a long and very arduous struggle, she survives. Yet she is paralyzed from the neck down with no realistic hope of recovering any further use of her limbs. She and her world are not the same. Moreover, they will never be the same.*

What is true for an individual can also be true for a group of people, even an entire nation. On September 11, 2001, people in the United States changed as a result of terrorism. They were *not* the same after mid-morning as they had been prior to that time. On September 12, 2001 and following, they began to realize that they and their world would *never* be the same.

When persons experience change as a result of a break in an attachment, they often look at the cause that has precipitated the break. Sometimes a break comes about by the action of an individual. At other times a break takes place without any clear indication of who caused it or why it occurred.

An infant sleeping in bed near a window is struck by a stray bullet. A child is diagnosed with leukemia. A teenager learns that she has an inoperable brain tumor. A man on the golf course is struck by lightning. A mother unknowingly contracts HIV. A grandfather develops Alzheimer's disease. A dump truck crosses the freeway median and hits a van carrying a large family head on.

Yes, *stuff happens!* And sometimes the cause is undetermined. And sometimes the reason why it takes place is simply unknown. Harold Kushner, in his book *When Bad Things Happen to Good People,* states a philosophical idea that he says is the key to everything else he is suggesting: "Can you accept this idea that some things happen for no reason, that there is randomness in the universe?" [2, p. 46].

To believe that there is a reason for everything that happens is a very heavy burden to carry. It means that an individual must always try to explain why something occurred. It also means that he or she will be frustrated by the inability to do so. And, worst of all, it means that an individual who believes in God will also believe that God must have a reason even when the reason is not apparent to the individual.

Furthermore, to believe that everything that happens is the will of God is an even greater burden to carry if one means by this that God is in charge of all that is going on in the world, day after day after day. For the result of such a belief is a great deal of frustration with God, even anger toward God.

An infant dies from a stray bullet. A child dies from leukemia. A teenager dies from an inoperable brain tumor. A mother dies from AIDS. A grandfather dies from Alzheimer's disease. A family of seven dies after their van is struck head on by a truck.

To understand the will of God in a more helpful manner is the goal of a brief, but important, volume written by Leslie Weatherhead, entitled *The Will of God* [3, 4]. In it the author distinguishes between God's intentional will (what is desirable from God's point of view), God's circumstantial will (what is possible for God given human choices), and God's ultimate will (what will still be accomplished by God in spite of human actions). Therefore, rather than ask whether a particular occurrence is God's will, one would ask whether such an occurrence is God's intentional will, God's circumstantial will, or God's ultimate will.

Weatherhead provides a number of illustrations in his analysis. Perhaps the most provocative is the crucifixion of Jesus where he states that it was God's intentional will that Jesus be followed by all human beings (God's ideal plan). However, since some human beings decided to kill Jesus rather than follow him, the crucifixion was God's circumstantial will (God's plan within certain circumstances). Yet, through the crucifixion, God accomplished God's ultimate will of redemption (God's final realization of God's purposes) by using the cross as the instrument to reach the goal God had in mind.

It is not easy to understand how God is involved with persons who are dealing with loss experiences, particularly when those experiences are devastating in effect and when the reasons why they are happening are unclear or even unknown. Yet, there are some basic beliefs about God that can be affirmed, beliefs that can empower persons to respond in some very wholesome ways.

The first of these beliefs is that God is good. It is captured in the responsive formulation: *God is good, all the time. All the time, God is good.* It is a statement about the character of God, namely, that God is inherently good, and that God's character does not change—regardless of what happens.

This means that when *stuff happens,* whatever it is, and however painful it is, one can depend on God being good at that very moment, and at every moment thereafter. Nothing can take place that will destroy the goodness of God—*nothing!*

The basis for this belief is the biblical record that contains Hebrew scripture (the first or old testament) and Christian scripture (the second or new testament). Passage after passage in each testament testify to God being good all the time. An example is in

Psalm 118. The first and last verses are identical: "O give thanks to the Lord, for he is good; his steadfast love endures forever."

In the second or new testament there is a related affirmation, namely, that Jesus Christ came to show us what God is like. Jesus came to reveal the goodness of God. He did this through his life, his teaching, his death, and his resurrection. Passage after passage testify to Jesus showing us what God is like. An example is in John 14:9. Jesus refers to God as Father and says, "Whoever has seen me has seen the Father."

There is also a second belief that can empower persons to respond in some very wholesome ways. It is that God works for good in everything. It can also be stated in a responsive formulation: *God works for good, in everything. In everything, God works for good.* It is a statement about the activity of God, namely, that God is working for good, and that God's activity permeates every situation in life—regardless of what happens.

This also means that when stuff happens, whatever it is, and however difficult it is, one can depend on God working for good at that very moment and at every moment thereafter. Nothing can occur that will stop God from working for good—nothing!

The basis for this belief is also the biblical record. The most explicit reference is Romans 8:28 in the Revised Standard Version (which is based on the most reliable manuscript evidence and which also provides the most accurate translation of the Greek text): "We know that in everything God works for good." Many other passages from both testaments also testify to this affirmation.

That God works for good in everything does not mean that God determines what happens or controls what takes place. God has given human beings freedom to choose and, in doing so, God has limited Godself (or himself, or herself—however the reader prefers to identify the reflexive pronoun) in such a way that God will not take away the freedom that God has given. In response to the question Kushner asks as to why bad things happen to good people, he says, "One reason is that our being human leaves us free to hurt each other, and God can't stop us without taking away the freedom that makes us human" [2, p. 81]. To underscore the importance of this claim, he also asserts: "I can only say that the cornerstone of my religious outlook is the belief that human beings are free to choose the direction their life will take" [2, p. 83]. He goes on to insist that "every adult, no matter how unfortunate a childhood he had or how habit-ridden he may be, is free to make choices about his life."

Many, many things happen in the world that are not good. God allows or permits them to take place. In doing so God limits Godself. God does this in direct correlation with the freedom God has given to human beings and to a variety of other forces in the world.

Such a limitation is voluntary on the part of God. It is God's choice. It is a choice that God could also withdraw. That is, God could unlimit what God has limited. However, God is dependable and can be trusted to function on the basis of the freedom that has been granted. In this God does not change. Therefore, God can be praised because God's character remains the same.

Although God's character does not change, God's activity does, since God interacts with human beings and with other forces in the world. Nevertheless, God works to bring about good in every situation in life. Therefore, God is always an ally, and never an enemy—regardless of what happens!

God is sovereign, yet God doesn't express God's sovereignty by determining all that takes place. God chooses self-limitation and, therefore, doesn't control everything, even though God could, and someday will—at the very end—when God acts to put a meaningful end to history. In the meantime, many, many things take place that are not God's will, if God's will is defined as what God wants.

Tyron Inbody, in his book entitled *The Transforming God: An Interpretation of Suffering and Evil*, makes a claim that he calls "the distinctively Christian answer to the problem of evil" [5, p. 188]. In his own words: "God does not will our suffering. God identifies with our suffering and works faithfully . . . to transform our suffering into the highest possible good" [5, 6]. This is certainly a valid claim; however, Inbody attempts to restrict this understanding to a process theology point of view. He does grant that Trinitarianism can also embrace such an understanding, though his delineation of Trinitarianism is also within a process frame of reference.

This "distinctively Christian answer" stated by Inbody is not restricted, however, in ways that he asserts. It is not limited to a process theology. It can be included in a theology of classical Christian Trinitarianism. Furthermore, it can also be included in a theology of non-Trinitarian theism such as is affirmed in Judaism, with persuasive arguments in support of it, particularly when one advocates a self-limitation on the part of God.

Such an interpretation of God—one who works faithfully to transform—is also at the heart of the point of view set forth in this volume. Furthermore, it can also be included in other views held by Christians as well as Jews and other traditions. For it asserts an understanding that is not necessarily limited to one particular theology.

Nevertheless, a belief in God—whatever that belief may constitute—is not a necessary constituent to transformation. For an individual is changed by responding to a break in an attachment, especially if he or she is not passive (letting things occur), but is active (choosing to respond to what has already occurred, or what is going to occur).

Whatever happens to an individual is influenced most directly by whether or not he or she chooses to respond in each of the phases in a wholesome manner (as identified in Chapters 3 through 6). This is at the core of a positive transformation. It involves choices, a considerable number of them, over a substantial period of time. It eventuates in a pattern of responses that form the level of transformation that occurs.

Those persons who consistently seek to bring good out of tragedy, even though they may deviate from doing so on occasion, often find wholesome ways to respond. This is the case for individuals as they deal with their own lives as well as when—as caregivers—they are relating to the lives of others. They focus their energy and their time on what they can do in response to what has already happened, or what is going to happen, even when they can't comprehend why the break in the attachment has occurred, or is going to occur.

This seeking to bring good out of tragedy is very significant in and of itself. That is, it is intrinsically valuable to function in such a way, even when one does not believe in God, or when one experiences God as an enemy. However, when one is able to add the dimension of God as one who is also seeking to bring good out of tragedy, he or she has an ally that can be enormously important as a source of strength and hope.

When one believes that God is working to bring about good, and even further, that God is working to do so in *everything,* then he or she can be affirmed in doing likewise. Furthermore—and this is the most exciting of all—one can even participate in what God is doing! Though, on the surface, this may sound presumptuous, it is not if it is done in a spirit of deep humility and gratefulness that one is privileged to share in such an undertaking.

A man sits and watches the evening news on his TV. As he does this he prays: "God, I believe you are working for good in the midst of all this tragedy." He watches some more. Then he prays again: "Help me, God, to understand how you are at work in one particular situation." He watches some more. Then he prays once again: "Help me, God, to find some way to participate with you as you work to bring about good in this situation."

This example illustrates the three steps in becoming a participant. The first is a statement of belief. The second is a request for understanding. The third is a petition to find a way to participate in God's work.

Steve Long, in his book *The Goodness of God,* concludes his analysis by stating that "our primary vocation is to bear witness to God's goodness" [7, p. 304]. He doesn't, however, define how this is to be done. He leaves it to his readers, if they do indeed choose to take up this challenge.

One does not need to reach the conclusion that Kushner does when he asks: "Are you capable of forgiving and loving God even when you have found out that He is not perfect, even when He has let you down and disappointed you by permitting bad luck and cruelty in His world, and permitting some of those things to happen to you?" [2, p. 148]. One can affirm that God does not need to be forgiven. Instead, God needs to be trusted in the midst of all the stuff that happens in life. And out of that trust, persons are called to bear witness to God's goodness, regardless of how deep the pain goes and how excruciating the pain feels.

God can be trusted *to be good* all the time and *to work for good* in everything, regardless of what takes place, regardless of how incredibly difficult it is, regardless of how unbearably painful it feels. Good *can* come out of tragedy. God *is* working to bring this about. Human beings *are invited* to participate in such a process.

While transformation takes place in all persons, however they respond to breaks in attachments, *there are possibilities that are available to each and every person* that can be very wholesome and, even further, very meaningful. And those possibilities emerge most powerfully when an individual gets in touch with his or her own resources for such transformation—a topic to be dealt with in the next chapter.

EXERCISES FOR READER
AND CAREGIVER

1. Review the exercise that you completed at the end of Chapter 6 in order to be reminded of the synthesis that you drew and the break that you identified.

2. **As a reader** who wants to integrate reading with self-understanding:

    a. Take a sheet of paper and record how you responded to the break you identified.

    b. Record what changes took place in your life as a result of the way you responded.

    c. Reflect on what you have recorded and see if there are insights that merge.

    d. Share your thoughts and your feelings with another person who is willing to listen and hear what you have to say.

3. **As a caregiver** who wants to understand someone else's life:

    a. Follow the same procedure for that person (on a separate sheet of paper) on the basis of how you experience that person. Proceed with caution.

    b. If the relationship is mutual and you want to understand the responses that each of you has made, and the changes that have taken place in each of your lives as a result of your responses:

        1) Invite the other person to follow the same procedure (on separate sheets of paper) that you carried out for yourself.

        2) Exchange comments in whatever sequence seems most comfortable.

        3) Try to understand each other's response, both intellectually and emotionally.

4. **As a caregiver** who wants to help others understand themselves, provide an opportunity for two or more persons to follow the same procedure. Use the guidelines given in the exercise at the end of Chapter 1.

5. Find other ways to adapt these exercises in creative and effective ways.

REFERENCES AND NOTES

1. T. Attig, *How We Grieve: Relearning the World,* Oxford, New York, 1996.
2. H. Kushner, *When Bad Things Happen to Good People,* Avon, New York, 1981.
3. L. Weatherhead, *The Will of God,* Abingdon, Nashville, 1944.
4. L. Weatherhead, *Why Do Men Suffer?* Abingdon, Nashville, 1936.
5. T. Inbody, *The Transforming God: An Interpretation of Suffering and Evil,* Westminster John Knox, Louisville, 1997.
6. P. S. Fiddes, *The Creative Suffering of God,* Clarendon, Oxford, 1988.
7. S. Long, *The Goodness of God,* Brazos, Grand Rapids, 2001.

CHAPTER 8

Resources for Transformation: Attachments

In the previous chapter the focus was on the claim that transformation takes place as one responds to a break in an attachment. It is inevitable. It always takes place. However, whether the transformation is basically positive or negative is largely up to the individual and the choices that he or she makes.

Every individual has resources available to him or to her in making such choices. As long as an age of accountability has been reached, and a physical or a mental condition has not impaired functionality, an individual can make use of his or her resources in responding to a loss.

A very significant step in this process is *the identification of one's resources*. They fall into two categories. First, there are resources within oneself. Second, there are resources beyond oneself; namely, one's attachments.

Understanding the resources within oneself is of paramount importance. For there is capacity within *each* person to deal with breaks in attachments, though some individuals are not in touch with this potential. Nevertheless, all persons can get in touch with it—sometimes with the assistance of a caregiver—even when it means unlearning some things that have been learned.

A woman becomes a widow very suddenly at age 36 when her husband is killed in an accident at work. She is left with four young children, all under the age of 10, and no income except for a small insurance settlement. She has had no job training and has never worked outside the home. After a few months of very intense grieving, she schedules an appointment with a counselor and shares that she sees no way to go on with her life. The counselor listens carefully and thoughtfully and helps her—over a period of weeks—to begin to realize that she does have the capacity to deal with the tragedy that has impacted her life so dramatically.

Understanding is necessary, though it is not sufficient. There must also be an actualizing of an individual's potential. That is, one must believe the capacity is there; one must want to bring it to fruition; and one must make a series of decisions based on this belief and this desire.

A man with a wife and three children, ages 7, 12, and 14, loses his job very unexpectedly due to a company buyout. He is overwhelmed and goes to talk with his pastor. He explains that he doesn't know what to do. He feels so dejected that he is not even able to go out and look for a new job. Through this meeting, and additional ones in the weeks following, he slowly becomes convinced that he probably does have what it takes to find a new position. He learns to accept more and more of what has happened, starts to contact prospective employers, and gradually becomes energized with the prospect of working once again.

It is still not sufficient, however, simply to act on the basis of what one believes and desires. It is also necessary to accept responsibility for making wise choices so that the result eventuates in a wholesome person who lives a meaningful life.

A young man in his mid 20s who is experiencing severe clinical depression comes to realize that he has been depending solely on his doctors to enable him to regain his health. He has been given medication upon medication over a period of many months. It also dawns upon him that he has not accepted any responsibility for regaining his own health. As a result, he decides to work with a team of medical professionals to see what he can do to help himself, as they do what they can. A gradual transformation takes place that significantly goes beyond what drugs alone were doing.

Central to this identification of resources within oneself is the capacity to trust oneself. It begins in infancy in the first stage described by Erik Erikson in his book *Childhood and Society,* as "basic trust vs. mistrust" [1]. In his own words, "The general state of trust . . . implies not only that one has learned to rely on the sameness and continuity of the outer providers, but also that one may trust oneself and the capacity of one's own organs to cope with urges" [1, p. 248].

Although identified in this initial stage, trust continues to be basic throughout all eight stages. In referring to his own chart of these stages, Erikson notes that "any line—horizontal or vertical—must be developmentally related to any other, whether in the form of an earlier condition or of a later consequence of demonstrable necessity" [2, p. 61]. This means that trust is the most foundational basis for any of the stages. It also means that subsequent stages cannot come to full fruition without it.

For Erikson there is also a virtue—an ego strength—that emerges out of each stage. For the first stage it is "hope." It comes out of trust. It is an understanding that Capps develops further in his identification of trust as the first and foremost ally of hope [3, p. 138]. In other words, where there is trust there is, or can be, hope.

Parkes also deals with trust in a significant way in an article entitled "Attachment, Bonding, and Psychiatric Problems after Bereavement in Adult Life" [4]. Building upon the work of Bowlby, he notes that "secure attachments in early childhood can be expected to give rise to a reasonable degree of trust in oneself with a reasonable degree of trust in others" [4, p. 271]. Out of these experiences of trust comes the confidence that enables persons to cope with breaks in attachments. Furthermore, as Parkes shows in his analysis, "self-trust" and "other-trust" are important determinants in *how* persons deal with breaks. A key conclusion he asserts is that persons low on "self-trust" are likely "to cling to others and to develop chronic intense grief" after a loss, while persons low on "other-trust" are likely "to withdraw and avoid situations which would evoke grief" [4, p. 278].

The subject of "self trust" has been further developed by Doris Brothers in her book *Falling Backwards: An Exploration of Trust and Self-Experience*. In it she distinguishes between four dimensions: trust-in-others (viewing others as trustworthy), trust-in-self (viewing oneself as capable of receiving trust from others), self-as-trustworthy (viewing oneself as a trustworthy provider for others), and others-as-self-trusting (viewing others as trustworthy providers for others) [5, p. 35].

In addition to the resources that one has within oneself, there are resources beyond oneself; namely, one's attachments (see Chapter 1). As the title of this chapter indicates, these attachments are resources that enable transformation to take place. Therefore, they are incredibly important!

The most helpful attachments are persons. This does not mean that things, places, events, and intangibles are not important. They certainly are. However, the most significant attachments are individuals and groups of individuals (assuming that one's attachments are reasonably wholesome human beings).

An elderly grandmother falls and breaks her hip. Her husband responds immediately and calls an ambulance. Her son and two daughters come to the hospital, as do the older grandchildren. Her rabbi and the president of the synagogue also come to see her since she has been a very faithful and devout member of the congregation for many, many years. Friends and neighbors follow. Plants and flowers come and keep coming. Cards fill a windowsill and a table in the room; the phone rings and rings. The response is almost overwhelming. There are so many persons who are important attachments.

The attachments that are stronger in degree are those that will be most resourceful. This is particularly true for persons to whom, and from whom, there is a strong attachment, some of which may also be considered affectional bonds (see Chapter 1).

A young man, age 15, goes into the hospital for tests to diagnose suspicious brain activity. Results a few days later lead to surgery to remove a suspected tumor. Surgery is lengthy and extraordinarily complex, leading to weeks of time in the intensive care unit and months of time in the hospital. Very crucial to him during this time in the hospital, and the many months of recuperation and ongoing treatment, are the very meaningful affectional bonds that he has with his mother and father, his older sister, and his grandparents on his mother's side.

Persons who are strong attachments must also be available if they are going to function as resources for transformation. This includes proximity, either in person or by some other mode of communication such as telephone or video phone, e-mail, or other mail. However, it also includes the circumstance of the other persons, particularly what is occupying their time and energy in significant ways.

A woman, age 42, is seriously injured in a car accident. Her husband, her lover, her best friend, a professor at the local university, has just arrived overseas in a remote area of Turkey with 27 of his students. They are on a three-week archeological trip in which they will visit numerous ancient sites and hear lectures from their professor at one or more locations each day. He tries—over and over again—to find a way to go home, but every plan he pursues doesn't lead to a viable solution. In addition, e-mail is not available and other mail is very slow. Only telephone contact is possible, though often not very reliable.

Persons who are strong attachments must also be suitable. This means they need to be reasonably wholesome and have some acquaintance with the break in attachment that the individual is experiencing. This does not mean that unfamiliarity prohibits resourcefulness, but it does mean that familiarity enhances the likelihood of resourcefulness, which, in turn, enhances the likelihood of transformation.

Parents are joyfully celebrating the wonderful experience that their 20-year-old son is having in a year-abroad program in New Zealand when they receive a shocking phone call. They are told that their son was killed in a car accident, that he died four days ago on a very remote road, and that his body was found only a few hours before the call was made. The parents are in shock, yet—somehow—they are able to make arrangements for the body to be flown home. They go through the motions of having a funeral, receive a great deal of care from others, but feel that no one really understands what they are going through. They do not have any opportunity to share with other parents who have experienced the death of a child. Months go by until they have a chance to talk with another set of parents whom they know fairly well who have also lost a child of a similar age and who are willing to talk about it. How different the conversation goes. How deep the experience is shared. How meaningful the attachment is. How helpful the conversation is.

It is highly likely that such attachments as those that have been described, particularly if they are affectional bonds, are persons that the individual can trust—deeply and unconditionally. And, because the quality of the trust is so meaningful, it generates a great deal of empowerment for the individual. It provides courage to face the break. It gives strength to work through the grief that results from the break. It enables hope to emerge!

A young couple in their mid-20s is looking forward to the birth of their first child. Baby showers are held. A bedroom in their home is newly decorated. Furniture, playthings, clothes, hygienic and nutritional aids are purchased and placed in appropriate places. The due date arrives. The baby doesn't seem to be moving. The parents go to the emergency room. Labor is induced immediately. The baby is stillborn. The parents are devastated—beyond description! Yet, in the midst of incredible grief, they turn to each other, to their parents and to their dearest friends—all close attachments that they trust very, very deeply. The intense anguish is not lessened, but genuine empowerment emerges in remarkable ways.

Yet, as profound as this is, it is not all there is. For there are other attachments that these attachments have. They also are reservoirs of empowerment, courage, strength, and hope. They sometimes flow to the individual through the attachments that are in closer relationship to the individual, but they also sometimes flow in a more direct manner, since they often include affectional bonds that the affectional bonds of the individual have. And when that occurs, the support can be incredible!

A single woman in her early 40s who adopted two sons in their infancy learns through a phone call from the police that her older son, a remarkable 16-year-old honor student, has been stabbed in the back while sitting on his bicycle at a street corner, waiting for the light to turn green. She rushes to the hospital to find her son already in surgery. Her parents and her sister join her shortly thereafter. They can't believe what has happened. And then, in the midst of their anguish and tears, the doctor approaches them and indicates that she and her staff did all they could to save his life, but were unsuccessful. Calls are made to other immediate family (who contact additional family members), to their closest friends (who reach out to other friends), to their priest (who gets in touch with several other members of the parish), and to neighbors (who call other neighbors and friends). As soon as they get home, visits begin, flowers arrive, and food is delivered, as attachments of attachments respond.

Yet, as significant as these additional attachments can be, there is still one more attachment that is—for the person who believes in God—the most profound of all. It is the attachment that will never be broken, unless the individual breaks it. It is the attachment that will *always* remain, unless the individual forsakes it. And it is the *only* attachment for which such a claim can be made!

This attachment is God, a claim that will sound presumptuous or at least ambiguous to some, yet quite meaningful to others.

A couple in their mid-30s is unable to become pregnant. They undergo in vitro fertilization three different times and finally a pregnancy occurs. About six months later premature twins are born. Their daughter only lives for 36 hours. Their son undergoes treatment after treatment, surgery after surgery, therapy after therapy, for many months, and then for a number of years. And through it all, the parents find enormous strength from their many close attachments, but none is greater than God, in whom they trust—more and more deeply—day by day, month by month, and year by year.

Such an attachment comes about as an individual responds to God's initiative, not the other way around. It is based on a belief that God reaches out to all human beings in a very caring manner, seeking to establish a relationship with each one. Yet God does not coerce an individual to respond. God respects the freedom that God has given each one to accept or reject God's caring initiative. Such a perspective is delineated in the volume by John Stackhouse, *Can God Be Trusted? Faith and the Challenge of Evil* [6, pp. 70-87].

God, who is good all the time and who works for good in everything (see Chapter 7), is attempting to establish a meaningful attachment with every human being. God is successful with some—those who respond to God's initiative—and unsuccessful with others—those who do not respond, those who live either unaware of this initiative, or unwilling to be receptive of it.

For those who do respond, the core element is trust. It is not unlike the trust that one develops with another human being. There is an introduction. There is a time of getting acquainted. A friendship develops. A significant relationship emerges. And throughout these stages trust emerges, deepening as time goes by.

So it is with God, though the process is often much more complex and often takes much more time. It may begin in infancy as an attachment to parents who trust God. It may continue as the infant grows into childhood and learns to trust his or her parents. As the child trusts the parents, who in turn trust God, the child learns to trust God. As years go by, and the child becomes a youth and realizes that if he or she is going to develop a mature religious sentiment, the trust in God must go beyond the faith of the parents. The youth must develop his or her own trust relationship with God—a relationship that will become tested over and over again, yet a relationship that can also deepen and deepen in trust.

Or trust may develop in ways that are not nearly as fortunate as the foregoing description indicates. It may not emerge until adolescence, or adulthood, yet may develop in significant ways in spite of, not because of, an earlier upbringing.

Furthermore, the pattern of a person's life is usually not so developmentally sequential. There are ups and downs of various kinds. There are times of mistrust as well as trust. There may even be periods of great turmoil—perhaps a number of them—periods that are so incredibly complex and tumultuous that trust in God doesn't even seem possible.

Throughout *whatever* may occur in an individual's life, God is nevertheless present. Carl Jung bore witness to this affirmation when he had the following words in Latin carved over the front door of his house in Zurich (words that were also inscribed on his tombstone): *Vocatus atque non vocatus, Deus aderit,* which in English means, "Called or not called, God is always there" [7, p. 56]. Or, to paraphrase those words, "Acknowledged or not acknowledged, God is still present."

The basis for this belief is stated in many passages in the biblical record. For example, in the first or old testament, the prophet speaks on behalf of God in Isaiah 41:10 and says, "I am with you." Or, in the second or new testament, Jesus says in Matthew 28:20, "I am with you always." In other words, God is always present, whether this is understood in Jewish terms, in Christian terms, or in some other terms.

Since God is good all the time, and since God works for good in everything, God can be trusted *to be* good and *to work for* good in each and every situation in which an individual finds himself or herself. God will never betray God's own character or the activity that takes place as an expression of this character.

Nevertheless, an individual may choose to break his or her attachment to God, even though God will never break the attachment to the individual. Or, an individual may experience a break in another attachment, and interpret that break to be caused by God, thereby interpreting it to be God's will. In that case, the individual may break his or her attachment with God and even become angry with God for being the cause of the break in another attachment.

A mother in her late 20s watches as her five-year-old son darts out across a country road and is struck and killed by a passing pickup truck. Her neighbor, in an attempt to comfort her, tells her—over and over again—that this is God's will. She goes on to state that God must have wanted her son in his garden and therefore reached down and plucked him up from this earthly garden. The mother loses her son and, at the same time, loses her relationship with God because she assumes God is the one who caused her son to die.

On the other hand, if an individual comes to realize that God didn't cause the break to occur, that it was not God's will (in the sense that this is what God wanted), then the break with God can be healed. In other words, the attachment to God that was broken by the individual, but not broken by God, can be restored. And when that takes place, God becomes an ally once again, rather than the enemy. Stuff did happen, but God didn't make it happen.

The same mother attends a Bible study at church that is led by the new pastor. After several weeks go by, she begins to question whether it really was God's will that her son was killed. She keeps remembering what her neighbor told her. She discusses her situation with her pastor and with other members of her study group. She begins to realize that the cause of her son's death may have been the passing pickup, or her son's carelessness, or her own negligence. She isn't sure, but she becomes fairly certain that it wasn't God who did this to her son. She begins, once again, to experience God as her comforter, her friend, her source of strength.

Besides identifying one's resources—a task that can be encouraging to those who have a number of meaningful attachments—there is another step in the process of responding to breaks in attachments. It focuses on *the utilization of the attachments that one has.*

In and of themselves, attachments can provide strength when one is faced with a loss that is coming, or that has already occurred. Furthermore, attachments can be a source of encouragement to a person who is working through the grieving process. In either case, they are important. For they are one's resources for transformation.

In relating to each other, attachments can often develop their own mutually supportive network of attachments. This is the value of one's own attachments having other significant ones. It increases the number of resources available to the individual.

A man in his mid-career is stunned and overwhelmed when he learns that his wife has died by suicide. He turns to those closest to him: his daughter, his son, his next-door neighbor of many years, and his supervisor at work. They each respond in very supportive ways. However, his daughter's new husband also responds together with his parents and other relatives. His son's many friends from church respond. His next-door neighbor contacts a number of other neighbors and they respond. His supervisor at work sends out a very thoughtful memo and a significant number of colleagues from work respond.

Furthermore, if some of the attachments that an individual has, and some of the attachments that those attachments have, each in turn also have an attachment to God, the potential for resourcefulness reaches a depth of meaning not otherwise available to an individual.

The same man also turns to his pastor who prays with him, meets with him a number of times, and, after getting the man's permission, shares the situation with the congregation at Sunday services and in the monthly newsletter. A variety of members visit with him in church or, on occasion, in his home. They invite him to join them for a meal at the end of a workday. They also include him in social gatherings. And, in many of these times together, they share their faith with each other in conversation, in prayer, and in corporate worship.

Over and above the identification and utilization of one's resources is a third step in the process of responding to breaks in attachments. It deals with *the determination of how the attachments will actually function.* This is rather easily done when the attachments are things, places, events, and intangibles. For the individual himself or herself decides. However, when the attachments are other persons, the situation is more complex.

Each attachment that is a person will have to decide what he or she will do. The individual can only nurture the relationship from his or her own perspective in as wholesome a manner as possible and trust those who are attachments to respond in a meaningful manner when a break takes place.

Likewise, the individual can only cultivate the relationship he or she has with God—if any at all—in as appropriate a manner as possible, and then trust God to respond and work for good in the situation where a break in an attachment is about to occur, or has already occurred. Over time the individual can become increasingly confident that God will do God's part—without having any reservations at all—just like the individual develops confidence that other persons will do their part. Eventually the individual may even come to the point of trusting God more deeply than he or she may trust any other individual, not only in life, but also in death.

Throughout the process of identifying, utilizing, and determining the functioning of one's resources runs the thread of trust: first in oneself, then in other persons, and ultimately in God. Trust is at the heart of all these dimensions of life. It creates meaning out of the past; it provides security in the present; and it serves as a springboard for hope in the future.

Trust comes, for some, to its most meaningful culmination in a relationship with God, whether one experiences this in a Jewish or Christian frame of reference, or in some other religious context. For it presupposes an experiential trust of oneself and an experiential trust of others. And, as meaningful as both of those dimensions are, it provides a depth of meaning that builds upon and surpasses them.

The writer of Proverbs in the first or old testament says in 3:5, "Trust in the Lord with all your heart, and do not rely on your own insight." The writer invites the reader to trust God with all of his or her heart, that is, with all of his or her being. The writer also asks the reader not to rely on his or her own insight. He does not say that the reader should not utilize all available insight. Rather, he recognizes that one's insight is sometimes insufficient and, therefore, cannot be solely relied upon. Therefore, he invites the reader to trust God always—in every situation that may arise in this life as well as in the experience that ends this life.

Resources for meaningful transformation are available to each and every person who experiences a loss, though some have far more access to such resources than others. Moreover, they can be plentiful to those who are willing to cultivate their attachments. Still further, they can be reliable to those who have learned to trust. And, when they are carefully and thoughtfully utilized, they can assist the individual in accepting his or her responsibility, in exercising his or her choice, and most important of all, in choosing a way of responding that will lead to a transformation that is emotionally healthy, intellectually coherent, spiritually genuine, culturally sensitive, relationally authentic, and personally fulfilling.

EXERCISES FOR READER
AND CAREGIVER

1. Review the exercise that you completed at the end of Chapter 1 so that you will be reminded of your attachments (as you perceived them at the time you completed the exercise).

2. Review the integrated visual summarization given in Chapter 1 so that you will recall the interactive nature of those attachments that are persons (arrows going out and arrows coming in).

3. **As a reader** who wants to integrate reading as well as exercises completed earlier with self-understanding:

    a. Take a sheet of paper and diagram your attachments once again. This time think about the attachments that you excluded, as well as included, when you did this exercise at the end of the first chapter. Try to make this new diagram a more accurate drawing of your primary attachments.

    b. Reflect on what you have recorded, making further modifications as insights emerge.

    c. Share your thoughts and feelings with another person who is willing to listen and hear what you have to say.

4. **As a caregiver** who wants to understand someone else's life:
   a. Follow the same procedure for that person (on a separate sheet of paper) on the basis of how you perceive that person. As you have done in earlier exercises, proceed with caution.
   b. If the relationship is mutual and you want to understand one another's attachments as fully as is reasonably possible:
      1) Invite the other person to follow the same procedure (on separate sheets of paper) that you carried out for yourself.
      2) Exchange diagrams and comments in whatever sequence seems most comfortable.

5. **As a caregiver** who wants to help others to understand themselves, provide an opportunity for two or more persons to follow the same procedure. Utilize the guidelines given in the exercise at the end of Chapter 1.

6. Find other ways to adapt these exercises in creative and effective ways.

REFERENCES AND NOTES

1. E. Erikson, *Childhood and Society*, pp. 247-251, W. W. Norton, New York, 1963 (revised and enlarged from 1950).
2. E. Erikson, *The Life Cycle Completed*, W. W. Norton, New York, 1997 (revised and enlarged by his wife, J. Erikson), wherein a ninth age is included.
3. D. Capps, *Agents of Hope: A Pastoral Psychology*, Fortress, Minneapolis, 1995.
4. C. M. Parkes, Attachment, Bonding, and Psychiatric Problems in Adult Life, in *Attachment Across the Life Cycle*, pp. 268-292, C. M. Parkes, J. Stevenson-Hinde, and P. Marris (eds.), Routledge, London, 1991.
5. D. Brothers, *Falling Backwards: An Exploration of Trust and Self-Experience*, W. W. Norton, New York, 1995.
6. J. G. Stackhouse, Jr., *Can God Be Trusted? Faith and the Challenge of Evil*, Oxford, New York, 1998.
7. V. Von Der Heydt, *Prospects for the Soul: Jungian Psychology and Religion*, Darton, Longman and Todd, London, 1976.

POSTSCRIPT

A Personal Story

It was a Friday evening. The date was May 10, 1996. I had just arrived home. Tears were already rolling down my cheeks as I opened the door. There stood my wife, Naomi, looking as distraught as I've ever seen her. We embraced immediately and sobbed in each other's arms.

I didn't want to let go, but I became aware of other people in the room. First I saw my pastor, Phil. We hugged as we cried. Then I saw my assistant from work, Sally, who is also Phil's wife. We also hugged as we cried. Then the doorbell rang and there stood my supervisor from work, Neal, the president of the seminary. We also embraced with tears flowing freely.

I don't remember any words that were spoken, except for those that Naomi and I shared as we recounted what we had heard. There had been a series of phone calls. The first one had come to Naomi at home. The message was that our daughter Bonnie had been hit by a vehicle and had been taken to the hospital. Details were unknown.

The message was immediately relayed to me in my office. It was after 4:30 P.M. The office was officially closed. I was reviewing words of tribute that I had written for a faculty colleague who was soon to retire and was being honored that evening. As I hung up the phone I went straight to the president's office to let him know that he might need to pinch-hit for me. I gave him a copy of what I had prepared.

As he was reviewing the text, his phone rang. He indicated Naomi was on the line and handed the receiver to me. I listened very intently as I heard her tell me she had just received another call from a family member in Indianapolis. "They've done all they can," she said, "but there doesn't seem to be any hope." I asked questions. Naomi answered as best she could, but she had been given very few details. Then she added, "I think they said they're going to try to keep her alive until tomorrow." My heart sank. I stopped breathing momentarily, and then burst into tears uncontrollably. I'll never forget that moment. "Then she's really died," I said to Naomi. "Uh huh," I heard in response.

I hurriedly left my tribute with Neal and asked him to present it on my behalf, but not to indicate what had happened. I didn't want to spoil the evening for my colleagues who were being recognized for their illustrious careers.

It was the details that we had heard in those phone calls that Naomi and I were now sharing with Phil, Sally, and Neal. It became clear to all of us—rather quickly—that Naomi and I needed to leave right away for Indianapolis, a trip of 210 miles.

The five of us decided to join together in prayer. We stood, formed a circle and held hands. And, as we were doing this, some words came out of my mouth without any forethought at all. I heard myself saying, "**Whatever happens, we're going to trust God.**"

I don't remember any other words that were spoken in that circle. Phil, Sally, and Neal probably said some very thoughtful things. They always do. Each of them probably prayed a very thoughtful prayer, but all I remember is that they were there. They had come right away. They had shown that they cared. They had joined with us in our excruciating pain.

I kept saying the words to myself over and over again, "Whatever happens, we're going to trust God." They were words springing up from the core of my being. They were comforting. They were strengthening. They were energizing. They served like an anchor to a boat caught in a raging storm.

The ride from Evanston to Indianapolis was very difficult, both intellectually and emotionally. The Friday evening traffic through Chicago was incredible. The usual trip of less than four hours took over five hours that night. As we slowly made our way through Chicago, we made calls to the hospital from our car. We began to put some pieces together. Bonnie had been struck by a city bus as she was crossing the street in downtown Indianapolis on her way home from work. She had lost consciousness immediately upon impact, had been taken to the hospital, had undergone surgery to explore the extent of injury to her head, had been diagnosed as unable to survive, and was being kept alive by numerous procedures, devices, and medications until we could get there, and until arrangements could be made for her organs to be donated and transplanted.

What made the ride even more difficult was the realization that she would probably be pronounced dead the next day, May 11th, my birthday. I sobbed and sobbed as I realized this. At times it was difficult to see the road through my tears. And, as if this were not enough, Naomi realized that Bonnie's death would come on Saturday, the eve of mother's day.

The details of the next 24 hours would take too long to describe in a postscript such as this. So much happened. So many people were involved. So much pain was felt.

After staying up all night and the entire next day, we concurred with the medical staff and joined them in pronouncing Bonnie dead at 6:15 P.M. Family members and a variety of caregivers joined Naomi and me in a large circle around the bed, committed her life to God, and prayed for the medical teams that would remove her organs and transplant them into others who were unknown to us.

Throughout those very, very difficult hours I found myself still trusting God in the midst of my pain. I hurt so deeply, yet I trusted God as deeply as I hurt. And, though I didn't expect it, my experience of intertwining the two became indescribably profound. Nothing was going to destroy my trust in God, not even the death of my beloved daughter.

Waking up in a strange hotel room on Mother's Day, Naomi and I could scarcely believe we would never see Bonnie alive again. The day before seemed like a dream, yes, a nightmare. Yet we knew Bonnie was dead. Even though it was hard to believe, it was true. Even though it didn't seem real, it was.

So much more happened on that Sunday as calls/flowers/visitors arrived, on that Monday when funeral arrangements had to be made, on that Tuesday when hundreds of people came to share in our grief, on that Wednesday when several hundred more came to attend the funeral service at Meridian Street United Methodist Church and to see her casket—now closed—at the front of the altar rail, the very location where she had been married ten months earlier.

Much more continued to happen in the weeks and months that followed. Yet, through it all, I didn't find myself feeling anger toward God for what had happened. I was angry with the bus driver for turning into a pedestrian walkway without paying attention, and for hitting Bonnie very forcefully as she crossed with the right of way on a green light, but I worked through that anger.

As the summer went on I found myself wondering if I was denying my anger toward God. I thought about it over and over again, very intentionally and very honestly. Was my repetition of the phrase, "Whatever happens, we're going to trust God," a way of not dealing with the harshness of what had happened? I thought about it very earnestly.

At the same time, I knew I'd faced harshness all of my life—directly, candidly, and in full view. I had learned that, for me, it made more sense to deal with reality just the way it was. Perhaps that's why Naomi and I went to the accident scene before we returned to Evanston, and stood at the edge of the street, with tears streaming down our faces, as we watched busses enter the pedestrian walkway precisely where Bonnie was killed. We wanted to face the stark reality of what had happened.

As the summer drew to a close, I began to realize—through my reflecting and praying—that something else had happened in my life years before. It was 20 years earlier, in 1976, that my other daughter Becky, at age 14, had been diagnosed with diplopia (double vision) and papilledema (a swelling of the optic nerve caused by a rise in pressure within the brain). That startling news also came on a Friday afternoon. And, by the following Monday, she was in the hospital for tests. Then, about a week later, she began a series of nine major surgeries. The first one tried to remove a growth that was blocking the fluid from moving through the ventricular system of her brain, but couldn't. A shunt was surgically placed to bypass the blockage. Eight more surgeries that followed dealt with a number of related problems, one of which was a massive subdural hemorrhage on the right side of her head (bleeding between layers of the brain). The threat of death came repeatedly. At one of those times, the doctors indicated they had done all they could and that we should be aware that she might very well die. It was so serious that we even began making funeral plans.

Becky was a very attractive person, an excellent student, and a leader in her school, in her youth group, and among her many friends. She was already becoming what her parents—and most parents—would want a teenager to be. And, then, very unexpectedly, her world changed. And so did mine, and Naomi's, and Bonnie's.

It seemed so unfair, so unfair. Why should Becky have such a blockage in her brain? Why should she have to undergo so many surgeries, so many treatments, and so many setbacks? Why should she have to spend over 140 days in one year in the hospital? Why should she have to be in ICU for week after week after week?

It was during these days of anguish on top of anguish that I began to question God more and more. It was not that I hadn't questioned God before. I certainly had—many times. Yet this time the severity of Becky's situation made my questioning much more intense. It was no longer in rather abstract philosophical or theological categories. It was no longer being carried out from a distance. It was no longer seen in the lives of other families. It was my daughter, my own flesh and blood.

I prayed for Becky. I prayed for her with Naomi. I prayed for her with others. I also asked others to pray for her, for those of us close to her, and for the medical staff who were working so diligently for her well being.

Yet one complication after another arose, and Becky seemed to be getting worse, not better. As a result of the massive subdural hemorrhage, she became paralyzed on her whole left side. She couldn't walk. She couldn't go to the bathroom. She couldn't feed herself. And her future became more frightening every day. Glimpses of sunlight came through once in awhile, but the clouds gathering over her life seemed to be getting darker and darker.

It all came to a climax for me one night after I got home from the hospital. I was sitting up by myself. Naomi had gone to bed. I felt such anguish and pain. At times I was in deep thought. At other times I was sobbing. And in the midst of it all, I found myself talking out loud to God—in order to stay focused—until it was almost dawn. It was a horrendous night. My tears flowed especially freely as I shared my anger with God, and more significantly, as I shared my anger toward God. I even said to God, "It's so unfair. I'm angry, even with you."

I had been told that God could take it. God did. God accepted my anger. God seemed to say that it was OK to be angry, even with Godself. Yet, I felt somewhat guilty for expressing such anger. But God seemed to reassure me that I didn't have to deny what I felt. I could express it and know that God would receive me and my feelings—just the way I was—even if God didn't deserve my anger.

I came to a deeper sense of trust that night than I had ever experienced before. I came to trust God in the midst of my anguish, my pain, and my anger. I came to trust God, regardless of what might happen in the future.

In the months and years that followed, that sense of trust deepened even further. I came to believe—really believe—that whatever would happen, I would trust God. I internalized this belief. It became a part of who I was.

Little did I know that 20 years later, while dealing with the shocking news that Bonnie had been struck by a bus and that she wasn't going to survive, that I would blurt out those words, **"Whatever happens, we're going to trust God."** Little did I realize that, when I wasn't angry with God after Bonnie died, that I wasn't denying my feelings, but was affirming what I had learned 20 years earlier.

Now I know that there is nothing that can or ever will destroy my trust relationship with God. It is an attachment—yes, an affectional bond—that is at the core of who I am.

Index